CLIMBING JACOB'S LADDER

LOUISE STOWE JOHNS

CLIMBING JACOB'S LADDER

12 STEPS IN YOUR SPIRITUAL JOURNEY

ABINGDON PRESS
Nashville

CLIMBING JACOB'S LADDER

Copyright © 1990 by Abingdon Press

This book is printed on acid-free paper.

Library of Congress Cataloging-in-Publication Data

JOHNS, LOUISE STOWE, 1942—

Climbing Jacob's ladder : twelve steps on your spiritual journey / Louise Stowe Johns.
    p.   cm.
    ISBN 0-687-08700-7 (alk. paper)
    1. Spiritual life. I. Title. II. Title: Twelve steps on your spiritual journey.
BV4501.2.J495   1990
248.4—dc20   89-48066
                                        CIP

MANUFACTURED IN THE UNITED STATES OF AMERICA

For
Dick, Evalyn, Christopher, Michele
All in prison

Soli Deo Gloria

PREFACE

I have received far more than I have given. Through my family, I have been and continue to be loved unconditionally. Among the people of God, I am nourished and challenged. From teachers and mentors, I have been given the space to create, and I have learned the discipline of intellectual inquiry.

To my friends in prison, especially at Julia Tutwiler Prison for Women in Wetumpka, Alabama, I extend my gratitude for sharing their lives with me, for their depth of insight, for having the courage to say, "I'm not sure I agree," and most of all for validating and accepting me. They have led me to places on my journey that I could never have imagined.

If these chapters can affirm those who have walked beside me, buoying me up in encouragement and in prayer, or those who have journeyed before me—if these words can return a portion of what has blessed me, I shall be thankful.

> The lines have fallen for me in
>   pleasant places;
> yea, I have a goodly heritage.
>   (Ps. 16:6 RSV)

Louise Stowe Johns

CONTENTS

The 12 Steps of A.A.

1. We admitted we were powerless over alcohol—that our lives had become unmanageable. **2.** Came to believe that a Power greater than ourselves could restore us to sanity. **3.** Made a decision to turn our will and our lives over to the care of God *as we understood Him.* **4.** Made a searching and fearless moral inventory of ourselves. **5.** Admitted to God, to ourselves, and to another human being the exact nature of our wrongs. **6.** Were entirely ready to have God remove all these defects of character. **7.** Humbly asked Him to remove our shortcomings. **8.** Made a list of all persons we had harmed, and became willing to make amends to them all. **9.** Made direct amends to such people wherever possible, except when to do so would injure them or others. **10.** Continued to take personal inventory and when we were wrong promptly admitted it. **11.** Sought through prayer and meditation to improve our conscious contact with God *as we understood Him,* praying only for knowledge of His will for us and the power to carry that out. **12.** Having had a spiritual awakening as the result of these steps, we tried to carry this message to alcoholics, and to practice these principles in all our affairs.

A NOTE TO THE READER

On any night in cities all over the United States and in other countries there is a meeting where people greet one another warmly, know one another's first name, and begin their formal time with prayer. It is not a revival or a Bible study, but the wisdom and insight that are the foundation of the meeting are easily transferable to a Bible study and to Christian nurture. For every meeting, the formula is the same: "Hi, I'm ———, and I am an alcoholic." The people understand and nod in agreement and self-awareness.

In this book, I am using the 12 Steps of Alcoholics Anonymous (AA). I join many others who have discovered the aptness of the steps to our lives, whether or not we have suffered a chemical addiction. It has been an exciting and fruitful alliance. The chapters in this book are most sensible when they are read in order, because the starting point is the awareness of our sinful state. We accept our weakness and God's power. But the experience of God's love for us and the grace extended by God keep this process from becoming a task similar to pushing a boulder up a mountain.

It was tempting to have one chapter for each step, but that would be a contrivance, causing superficiality in steps that warranted more depth. Step 1 in AA requires an admission of powerlessness over alcohol. Other self-help groups that use the 12 Step program have inserted their own addictive substance in place of alcohol: drugs, food, emotions, and others. The second and third chapters point out our lack of power. Until we put ourselves under the authority of God, our lives will be unmanageable. In one we learn of the dawning awareness of faith by a Roman officer and in the other, conversations with sheep help us to examine humorously our own foibles. In chapter 5, "Waiting for the Light to Shine," I have chosen to compress five of the steps. This was done because the actions that are invited are tightly interwoven: to examine one's conscience without confession and petitioning God for removal or change of the shortcomings is to leave loose spiritual ends. Chapter 6 continues work on steps three through seven by looking at the way Jonah handled God's grace, extended toward Gentiles. The final step, which tells of the joy of a spiritual awakening finding expression in service and in living the good news is certainly worth at least two chapters (11 and 12).

One Sunday, the story of Jacob and the ladder showed up in the lectionary. Later, a brief article in *Modern Liturgy* by Kenneth Guentert suggested parallels between the 12 Steps and Jacob's vision (see Kenneth Guentert, "Final Blessing: Jacob's Ladder," *Modern Liturgy* 14 [Summer, 1987]: 38). It was the beginning of a provocative and stimulating alliance that has pushed and pulled me into greater depth and greater extension of my own spirituality. May it be the same for all who risk the steps.

Louise Stowe Johns

CLIMBING JACOB'S LADDER

We are climbing Jacob's ladder,
We are climbing Jacob's ladder,
We are climbing Jacob's ladder,
Soldiers of the cross.

ONE

A LADDER INTO BETH-EL /
GATEWAY TO GOD

Jacob, the twin brother of Esau, was the second son by a turn inside the womb, and within the womb sibling rivalry was already underway!

> And Isaac prayed to the Lord for his wife, because she was barren; and the Lord granted his prayer, and Rebekah his wife conceived. The children struggled together within her; and she said, "If it is thus, why do I live?" (Gen. 25:21-22*b* RSV)

Born to Rebekah and Isaac, Esau pleased his father with the results of his hunting. Jacob won his mother's heart and found pleasure in being at home. Esau was apparently not the most astute or discerning person in his youth. He allowed emotions to overtake reason and succumbed to the plans of a calculating mother and an aspiring younger brother.

Jacob took advantage of Esau in a weak moment, and the birthright due Esau was sold to Jacob—for a bowl of vegetable soup! Then deftly assisted by his mother, Jacob lied to Isaac, and thus secured the blessing that was also intended for Esau. Esau was livid that his brother and mother had played on Isaac's infirmities of age, and thereby denied Esau the blessing He promised himself that he would kill his brother, Jacob. By Rebekah's contrivance of getting Jacob out of danger (with an additional blessing from Isaac!), Jacob was sent to Paddan-aram to look for a suitable bride. Again Esau had apparently been outwitted.

If Jacob had possessed the insight of people yet unborn, he might have known better. When you think you are running away, you can run smack into God. Generations later, Moses faced God unexpectedly at the burning bush (Exod. 2). Elijah was confronted by God in a cave (I Kings 19). Each was surprised by God while trying to escape from a precarious predicament, threat of death, and avoidance of responsibility.

On the run, Jacob was alone and vulnerable, a fugitive from Esau's justice. If wild animals didn't get him, nomads probably would. But when you have traveled all day, and night is on you, the safest thing to do is stop, build a fire, and try to get some sleep. Lying down that night with a stone for a pillow, Jacob dreamed a most remarkable holy vision. In his dream, he saw a ladder, connecting earth with heaven, and angels were going up and down it.

And God spoke to Jacob, the man more comfortable in the tent than on the hunt, the man least likely to succeed in the wilds. God said: "I am your God and the God of your ancestors; the land will be yours and more besides; your family will be great! I make this promise as one that I will fulfill, not leaving you until all of what I have promised has been accomplished" (Gen. 28:13-15, paraphrased).

When Jacob awoke, he affirmed the reality of the dream. He declared, "God was surely in this very place, and I had not even expected it, nor sought it! This must be the house of God, and I have slept at the gate of heaven!" (Gen. 28:16-17, paraphrased). Jacob did what was externally correct: he consecrated that gate to heaven by pouring oil over his stone pillow and naming it Beth-el: the house of God.

In the dream, Jacob was not invited to ascend the ladder or to speak. Although the ladder clearly brought heaven within reach of earth, it was not for Jacob's use. Not one step did he take onto the ladder. It was a setting for showing God's glory, for ascent and descent of the angels, to establish a connection between earth and heaven. The fear and awe Jacob felt were that of a person overcome with the presence of the most holy. Jacob was not so overcome, however, that he lost his ability to make a deal. He told God that if God would take care of him (as God had already promised in the dream) and restore Jacob in peace to his home, then Jacob would declare Yahweh to be his Lord and give to Yahweh one tenth of what was given to him.

What a night! Jacob, the opportunist, the trickster, the liar, was an unlikely candidate to meet God and to receive not God's condemnation, but God's blessing, which both echoed and far outshone the blessing Jacob stole from Isaac.

For a person like Jacob, who is at the bottom of the ladder, there is the option of either turning aside or believing in and accepting the full life offered. Acceptance necessitates action or steps. The 12 Steps, originating with Alcoholics Anonymous—which was founded in 1935—but widely used by other similar self-help groups, has insightful parallels for a person at such a crossroads.

As a prison chaplain, working with many persons whose lives have been devastated by chemical addictions, I have gained an appreciation of the spiritual wisdom and spiritual dimensions of the 12 Steps.

In summary, the first three steps say, "I can't. God can. I'll let God." But don't discount the wisdom if you do not have an addiction to alcohol or another substance. Easily, each and every one of us can say: I admitted I was powerless over sin, that my life had become unmanageable. The steps recognize how upside down our world becomes when our pride and inflated ego take on godlike proportions.

On that night, when Jacob was alone in the wilderness, he faced God and God's glory. Jacob realized his own personal inadequacy, affirming a need for God. Jacob was at the bottom; there was no invitation in the dream for him to ascend the ladder. Instead, he was to meet God in a way he had never experienced before, and it placed him on the brink of changing his life forever.

We have all been on the verge of change. In the story of the healing of the centurion's servant in Luke 7 and Matthew 8, the centurion exhibited the belief that Jesus could heal the centurion's slave.[1] Jesus praised that faith! What happened next in the centurion's life? Was his allegiance to Roman gods supplanted by a new belief? We do not know. What happened to Jacob, on the brink of incredible potentiality, we can follow in the Scriptures. The centurion and Jacob were at the bottom of the ladder—with so much to gain and nothing to lose. However, believing in God is not enough.

Approximately 90 percent of Americans believe in God—a "higher power." No one would say that those 90 percent predicate their lives on that belief. Ninety percent of the American people do not make decisions on and live by the teachings of the Bible or other holy scriptures. I make these observations because the reminder is important. Belief in God does not mean embodiment of that belief. We are painfully aware of that fact when a professing Christian fails to act in a Christlike manner. But we must guard against the luxury and smugness of pointing fingers at all our acquaintances, friends, and enemies about the paucity of their belief as compared to the sureness of our own religious state. We should search ourselves vigorously.

The journey I want to describe can be aptly illustrated by two concrete entities: the ladder and the spiral. The ladder, as in Jacob's dream, is the earth-heaven connection. It is easy to discern progress on the ladder. The ladder allows us to distance ourselves from the business of the earth, which binds us and holds our loyalties. When we climb stairs, if we have the energy and the leg stride, we can take several at a time, but we don't jump them all at once (unless it is on the way down!). For each of us, going up is a daily process, climbing higher and higher toward God. But the verticality of the ladder image is inadequate. A three-dimensional spiral can suggest moving from plane to plane. As we go out or in, spiraling beyond or spiraling within, our faith deepens and expands. We experience and know God beyond us, beside us and within us, and we find our true selves in the "higher Source within."[2] A one-dimensional life can be like drawing a circle on paper and returning again and again to retrace the figure. Each time the lines become more deeply embedded, lessening the probability of escaping the malaise. But the spiral is an image of the repetitive nature of life, which does not endlessly repeat the exact same mistakes or successes: each bend or turn of the spiral has a unique aspect of its own, with the opportunity for progress.

In dance, there is a movement called the tripudium: three steps forward, then one step backward. The ancient Romans performed this dance as a way of demonstrating humility and reverence: "I go forward, yet I falter."[3] In AA, one could mistakenly presume that once a step has been taken or worked, the content of that step might be forgotten. Any honest recovering addict will quickly correct the deception in such thinking. We will either sink by the weight of our own sins or with courage and determination repeat the steps. As in the tripudium, we can make progress, although we falter momentarily.

His audience with God put Jacob in an enviable position. He had everything he could have wanted. It would be downstream from then on! With God's promises and protection around Jacob, his life would be better than that of a storybook character.

No, not exactly. Jacob's early life appears to have been the tripudium in reverse—one step forward, three steps back. But the dream was God's offer to Jacob to begin his journey.

Jacob traveled many more miles, lived many more years, lost and regained the vision, grew in his faith, and learned how to live in a faithful way before his progress on the spiraling ladder reached its deepest and greatest extension. Remember, the awareness of God's presence and God's being is the beginning of the journey, not the end.

How we perceive others in relation to the ladder is revelatory of our perspective. Speaking of others "at the bottom" graphically asserts superiority over those below us. This may be a way of forgetting that we all start out at ground level. The person who has recently been born again, the person who makes a first-time profession of faith, and the infant in Christ all start out at ground level. A person's chronological age only hints at his or her possible spiritual maturity. When we say that we believe, our journey begins. Wherever we are on our spiraling ladder, one hand can steady us. The other should be out, helping those who are behind or seeking help from those who are ahead. Helping, seeking, steadying—all intertwine.

Jacob had come into the presence of God, and he confessed that God is. Jacob recognized the existence of a power greater than his own. Jacob had lived as one in a cocoon, totally absorbed and contained with pleasuring himself. But he had a vision that convinced him of God's sovereignty in his life and in the universe.

Where are you on the spiral? You do not need to wait for a spectacular dream to make the decision of whether to climb the ladder, growing closer to God and becoming your original self, which has been tarnished by sin. Jacob's dream demonstrated that God was willing to come to him. A god who can stand beside us is a god who is accessible and unafraid of mingling with mortals. If you decide to acknowledge God's supremacy in your life, you will find that God waits for you as well.

In the junior high church camp I attended, the last group activity for each day was for all the campers to form a large circle under the stars, holding hands and joining their feet to the earth. We walked slowly around as we sang "We Are Climbing Jacob's Ladder." Melodically, this song progresses upward, until it drops back to earth and hard reality to the line "Soldiers of the cross." But there is assuarnce and hope in the spiritual as "Every round goes higher, higher." In that second verse, unexpectedly, a spiritual with obvious verticality in its ladder theme becomes cyclical: the resolute journeyer goes up and around.

On those evenings, I sensed a fullness of time. Now I understand that the music on the breeze of a summer night carried us back to Jacob's vision and invited us to join Jacob on every round.

A folk song collapses the time between Jacob and Jesus, as

Jesus becomes the ladder of mercy and grace, raised up for each of us.

> As Jacob with travel was weary one day,
> At night on a stone for a pillow he lay;
> He saw in a vision a ladder so high,
> That its foot was on earth and its top in the sky.
> Alleluia to Jesus, who died on the tree
> And has raised up a ladder of mercy for me,
> And has raised up a ladder of mercy for me.[4]

NOTES

1. See chapter 2, "A Gentile's Faith," for a fuller discussion of the centurion.

2. Edward Hoffman, *The Heavenly Ladder; The Jewish Guide to Inner Growth* (San Francisco: Harper & Row, 1985), p. xi.

3. Marilyn Daniels, *The Dance in Christianity: A History of Religious Dance Through the Ages* (New York: Paulist Presss, 1981), p. 33

4. *Supplement to the Book of Hymns,* Supplemental Worship Resources II (Nashville: The United Methodist Publishing House, 1982), no. 859. The words are by an anonymous writer and the music a traditional folk hymn.

In chapters 2 and 3, it is admitted that we are powerless over sin and that our lives are unmanageable.

TWO

A GENTILE'S FAITH

I was listening to a translator as he endeavored to convey meaning from Russian to English. I also listened to the Russian and was impressed with a parallel to Bible study and faith. The Russian spoke with emphasis, emotion, and passion. The interpreter objectively conveyed words, but controlled the expression of feelings. The natural rise and fall in voice patterns was missing. Fascinated by that awareness and wanting to test it with other translators, I began craving newscasts in which an interpreter could be heard as well as the native speaker. As I expected, for many interpreters the style was the same: the translator did not let emotions color the transmission. That is both understandable and regrettable.

The printed pages of a translated Bible are our interpreter of the original language and of the original emphasis and emotion. Reading from the Bible or hearing the Bible read becomes a thirdhand experience if we are not deliberate in our efforts to get back to the joy, pain, excitement, puzzlement, or any other responses of a firsthand presence.

One way to overcome the flat, two-dimensional quality of the thirdhand objectivity is to flesh out biblical personalities by conversing with them. Time and space need not be deterrents. With imagination and knowledge of the times of the Bible, we can step into the stories. We can be touched and changed, and then discover that much of what motivated and moved our

Jewish and Gentile sisters and brothers moves and motivates us even today.

I invite you to go back with me to a day in the city of Capernaum, a fishing harbor that was the center of Jesus' Galilean ministry. From three different perspectives we will hear the important story of a foreigner's faith. Only one named character in this retelling is not a part of the biblical account in Luke 7:10.[1] I have named her Sarah. The centurion is a central figure in the story and deserves the name I have given him, Justus.

Jesus was entering Capernaum, the city that felt like home to him. He and his followers were enjoying the lake breeze, unconcerned with the report that was delivered about their presence.

Soldiers brought the word to the centurion Justus. "That Jewish teacher, Jesus, is back in town. The crowds are already gathering. Shall we take care of them?"

Justus tried to focus his thoughts on their report. He was absorbed with thought of the critical illness of the child, Josiah. Justus was well aware of Jesus. They had kept a close watch on him, especially after he taught in the synagogue, then healed the possessed man. Jesus might be a threat to the peace in Capernaum, but the accounts of activities thus far didn't paint the picture of a troublemaker.

"He usually stays with the mother of Simon, one of his followers," Justus commented. "Does the Rabbi appear to be going in that direction?" Without waiting for a reply, Justus continued, "I desire no conflict with the teacher nor with the Jewish elders." Then Justus sent the soldiers away, saying, "Keep an eye on Jesus, but no confrontation! I believe he means no harm."

The soldiers departed, and Justus was immersed again in his despair over Josiah. "Josiah is at the point of death. For days he has tossed and turned, sweating through his clothes and the blankets as the fever will not break or leave him. Now the child lies motionless. For hours, they say, he has not opened his eyes or moved his lips. I don't really care if they saw my tears as I knelt by his bed, trying to give him some of the life-strength that is within me. I've never hidden my affection for Josiah, my slave.[2]

"All my wisdom fails me now. The cures of the Roman doctor are of no use. I have called on our gods for days and nights without end, but they, too, are impotent. In this land of the God of Abraham and Sarah, the God of the Jerusalem Temple and synagogue, should I call on that God?"

Justus' thoughts ceased, and he dropped his head. Then, as one inspired, he looked up and spoke aloud. "What a fool I am! My soldiers only moments ago reported that the healer, Jesus, has come into town. Preoccupied with Josiah, I didn't put it together. If the Rabbi can cure that possessed man, why can't he heal my servant?" Justus paused in a moment of self-awareness. "But who am I to a man with so much power?" Then his confidence returned. "I know I am unworthy of Jesus' goodness and any act of kindness, but we do have one thing in common: I am accustomed to giving commands and having them obeyed, as is the Rabbi. I believe that all Jesus has to do is to give the order and my servant will be healed. I have shown my respect for the Jews by building them their synagogue. Now I will ask them to plead my case to Jesus."

Jewish elders of Capernaum brought to Jesus their plea on behalf of Justus. Jesus was moved by their compassion and by their concern, which rose above nationality and overcame status of conquered and conqueror.

As Sarah walked from the market with fruit and bread for her family, she was irritated about the man whose name evoked varying reactions. "This man Jesus is getting to be a nuisance in our town," she thought. "He acts as if he had been born here! But he wasn't. Being born in Bethlehem, then growing up in the little town of Nazareth, maybe he doesn't know himself where he's from, or where he wants to be from! It's quite enough to have a Roman garrison with the soldiers acting as if they own the town! Whatever they think in Rome, across the sea, we Jews own this town: no tax collector, centurion, or emperor can change that! Some of them try to appear as if they care about us. It seems to have impressed plenty of folk here that Justus gave so much money to build us a synagogue. I don't care how many soldiers he commands. I see right through him: our good will makes his job in our city much easier."

Sarah was tiring from her walk with the heavy load and the energy she had expended as she fussed about Jesus and the Romans. Absorbed in those concerns, she was unaware that she was approaching a crowd.

"What now?" she said aloud. Coming to the edge of the crowd, she could barely see the elders of the synagogue talking with someone. "Why the commotion?" she asked a man standing near her.

"I can't tell for sure," he answered. "They are asking the Rabbi Jesus something, but we are too far back to make it out."

"Why doesn't he leave well enough alone?" Sarah responded without thought.

The man looked at her incredulously, "Have you heard him speak and teach? Do you know that the demons obey him and that he can restore people to health? He surely is a prophet from God!"

There was only time for Sarah to reply with a defiant, "Magic!" when report of the conversation reached them. "Justus, the centurion, has a slave who is near death. He wants Jesus to go and heal his slave. The elders say the centurion loves our nation, that he deserves Jesus' acting to save the life of the slave."

By now the crowd was moving along with Jesus, heading straight for Justus' home. Sarah thought she had heard and seen enough and started away from the curious, then changed her mind. "Let's see how he handles this tool of the Romans. That will tell us a lot about who and what he is." So she reversed her direction, catching up with the crowd.

Ahead, Sarah could see people coming to meet Jesus. He stopped and spoke with the three who had come. "Jesus doesn't appear to be mad or upset or to be telling them how awful the Roman tax is," Sarah's voice betrayed her disappointment.

Jesus turned from the men and said in a strong, clear voice to the expectant crowd, "The centurion who lives among you, a man of authority and position, has such faith as I have not seen in all of Israel."

The crowd was stunned! "What did the man say to Jesus?" Sarah inquired again and again. No one had heard. Jesus moved away from the crowd, some of his followers close behind.

The next day, after Sarah heard that the centurion's slave had been healed, she boldly professed, "A magician—not a prophet of God!".

Sarah chose to be thirdhand in her response to Jesus. Her self-concern made her own passions the most important; therefore, she was unable to identify with anyone else. Justus, in stark contrast, plainly and loudly declared his faith and acted on it.

From the story, we learn about Justus' character, which was commendable and created the environment in which Jesus' power could be manifested. Justus respected persons, no matter what their status in life. His servant was dear, or valuable, to him. This could have been an economic concern, but the entire story mitigates against that interpretation. It is from the testimony of the elders who went to Jesus that we learn that Justus was a worthy man who loved their nation. Then they tell of his building the synagogue for the town. Justus' respect for the beliefs of others was visible to the inhabitants of Capernaum in the form of the synagogue that he built.

The position of centurion, in command of one hundred soldiers, carried with it prestige and power. Justus understood his power, and he understood the limits of his power and authority. Equally as important, he was willing to declare that to Roman and Jew alike. He did not send for Jesus in the middle of the night, swearing his soldiers and household to secrecy. His action was at once courageous and humble.

The Bible is full of unexpected protagonists, and the centurion joins those ranks. Those with whom Jesus associated day after day would be expected to believe in him, as many did. Those who witnessed a miracle, heard Jesus' teaching, stayed near him a while could be expected to have faith. But it is likely that Justus never heard Jesus preach, and until Jesus' healing of his slave, never felt the power of his working a miracle. Reports must have varied greatly, from the type of response Sarah had of his being a magician to his being called an impostor. Apparently the centurion allowed the inspiration of the Spirit of God to lead him.

The story of the centurion is one of many intriguing mysteries in the Bible. Did the centurion become a Christian, or was that one incident in his life in which he had no clear understanding of what motivated his decision? How did his urgent plea for help from Jesus affect his authority over his garrison and the Jewish elders? Truly he was at a crossroads. Perhaps for only a moment in his life he understood that Jesus' power and authority were greater than his authority over the soldiers, and thereby over Capernaum, greater than Roman medicine, greater than Roman gods. The faith foundation was there for discipleship, proclaimed clearly by Jesus himself. But we do not know whether the centurion's belief was in one who could call on the gods and perform a miracle or in one who is the Son of God.

I hope that the centurion became an example for all in that city, that his influence lasted as did the physical evidence of his generosity in the synagogue. Speaking to us today across the centuries, he could respond to questions about what led him to seek Jesus' help and whether that changed his life. I think he might answer, "When I realized the limits of my own capabilities, I was open to acknowledging a power greater than mine. On that day, when I understood clearly that my gods and my efforts had no potency to effect anything, I felt an indescribable peace because I realized that I was not in control of a hundred soldiers or a city or even myself. My life was forever changed because I began to open myself to God. I let God's leading be what directed my life, and that transformed my will into God's will."

Attesting to God's greatness has little significance when uttered by a person with either low self-esteem or an inflated ego. I am at my spiritual strongest when I am neither wallowing in self-abnegation nor reveling in delusions of grandeur. When I see myself as a person of worth in God's eyes, a person for whom God would send a Savior, I also see a God far, far greater than I. In awe I humbly bow before God, but my spirit is elevated, glorifying God!

> When [Jesus] was not far from the house, the centurion sent friends to him, saying, "Sovereign, do not trouble yourself, for I am not worthy to have you come under my roof; therefore I did not presume to come to you. But say the word, and let my servant be healed. For I am a man set under authority, with soldiers under me: and I say, 'Go,' and he goes; and to another, 'Come,' and he comes; and to my slave, 'Do this,' and the slave does it." When Jesus heard this he marveled at the centurion, and turned and said to the multitude that followed, "I tell you, not even in Israel have I found such faith." And when those who had been sent returned to the house, they found the slave well. (Luke 7:6b-10 ILL)

NOTES

1. Luke 7:1-10. Another version is in Matthew 8:5-13. John 4:46-53 can also be compared.

2. Although the text does not state the age or sex of the slave, I have chosen to think of the slave as a male child.

THREE

LET'S HEAR IT FROM THE SHEEP

Sheep and shepherds, shepherds and sheep. When we hear those words in a church setting, the connections are immediate: Jesus is the good Shepherd, and we are the sheep—with tendencies to go astray. Allusions in both the Old and the New Testaments to sheep, as well as descriptions of unscrupulous shepherds and loving shepherds, were easily understood by the Middle Eastern people, whose culture and economy centered around sheep. Since the metaphors come from real people and real animals, I thought it would be enlightening for us to visit some sheep and a shepherd to get their views on the state of shepherding and "sheeping."[1]

Jacqueline is our first sheep to speak.

Being a sheep is not my idea of fun, because the shepherds never seem satisfied. On a regular basis, we get a shearing. Lambs always get it first! I can tell when it's nearing time for a shearing because we get bathed with that stinky sheep-dip. Then they start coming at me with their sharp-edged tools; it makes me really nervous. They can't all be experts in fleecing. What if I get cut! I personally am very attached to my woolly coat. Why do I have to give my wool up so that someone else can have socks or a fancy sweater? I think it is selfish for them to take my hair for their comfort or haute couture. And who wants to be turned into a diploma?

I'll tell you what I can't stand: those things masquerading as sheep with curled-horns and broad tails! Just look at me and my beautiful short tail and short, fine wool. No one cuts off my horn or my tail so they can use the tail for cooking fat or the horn for a flask! They say they're sheep; maybe they are, but I have my doubts.

After the shearing, it's party time for everyone—except us. They have a big meal and count their shekels. I have it on good authority that alpacas have beautiful long, silky hair. So my suggestion is to write an alpaca-herder in Peru and do a little fleecing. Shouldn't we share this honor? Here am I, but, fleece the alpacas!

There is nothing sheepish about Jacqueline! Do you detect a lack of generosity and an abundance of self-absorption in her? Is it possible that sheep can be prejudiced?

Let's listen to Randall. He's a veteran in the flock shepherded by Michele.

We have such a picky shepherd. She counts us all the time. If you wander the least little bit beyond the sheepwalk, she's right on you, using that crook. I fell once and was perfectly capable of righting myself. But oh, no! Up she runs, reassuring me with that irritating voice of hers, and she gets me back up! What about a sheep's dignity?

She wants us to be in the sheepcote by a certain time each night. I find that really boring! If you ask her—or one of the others who have sold out to her, like Stephen—why, they say, "Because there are wolves and lions and snakes and jackals and bears! You could be torn from limb to limb! You might fall into a pit." That's only a scare tactic. I've been around long enough to know better. Oh, sure, you see a snake or a jackal on occasion (especially if you are woolgathering), but get real: she wants absolute obedience from us. Whether we live or die, she doesn't care. It's a power thing, and Jacqueline will back me up on that! Our shepherd has to have her own way, and she is totally unconcerned about our feelings. They always finish their lecture, those sold-out sheep, saying, "It's for your own good." I'd like to make that decision for myself! I'm no lamb. No one should be telling me what to do!

I'm just waiting for a time when I can make my own decisions.

And that can't come soon enough—no bosses, no fleecing, no whiny, wimpy, sold-out sheepsheads!

I would say that is one hostile sheep! Perhaps Miriam will help balance our sheep snapshot. She comes from another flock and will give us a different perspective.

I can take our shepherd—or leave him. Mind you, he doesn't know that. He thinks I'm devoted to his every move, his every direction. I stay quite still while he pulls the burrs from my short, thick wool. I know and "obey" his every word. When I want to have a little fun, I pretend to get caught in the brush, or I head toward the sheepkill. He always comes rushing to my aid. I have him trained all right!

Sometimes when I think our shepherd isn't paying much attention to me, I just make sheep's eyes at him. It gets him without fail! I have him fooled, and that is where I plan to keep him!

So far, this has not been the most appealing collection of sheep. We've gone from self-centered to hostile. Miriam would qualify as a con-artist. I've had my eye on Stephen for a while. I believe we'll hear a different attitude from him.

We have a new shepherd. When she first took over the flock, we were badly scattered and frightened. Three had been killed by wolves. Others had been taken away in a raid by Bedouins. Many were lost; we don't know what their fates were. I know that some of them were cranky and hard to get along with, but I miss them. Our shepherd searched for every sheep that was lost from our flock and brought back all that were still alive. Those that had been hurt, she didn't leave to die but tenderly nursed them.

Finally we are together again, with the water and protection we need. We are safe and well-fed, but not fat! I sure don't want to be one of those sheep that does whatever it pleases, pushing around the weaker sheep, never obeying the shepherd. Those sheep get soft and lazy. When necessary, the shepherd separates those sheep from the rest of us, and we never see them again.

Our shepherd is strict because she knows what we need, and

she provides it. When we put ourselves in a stupid situation, acting the sheepshead, she always wants to be sure that we know why what we did was wrong. But when we try to do better, she is very loving and encouraging, giving us another chance. She disciplines us when needed with her gentle strength that is an expression of her heart.

On two occasions, she saved my life. Both times I was within inches of our mortal enemy, the snake. Just as the snakes coiled to strike, she struck them with deadly blows of her rod. I was very shaken, but the shepherd reassured me by speaking to me in a soothing tone. After a while, I felt better. I guess you could say that I love my shepherd. Maybe sheep aren't supposed to have those feelings, but I do.

While we are on an upswing after hearing from Stephen, let's hear from Michele, the shepherd for Jacqueline, Randall, and Stephen.

As a herder of sheep, it is quite distressing for me to see the sheep scattered, hurt, dying, or dead. I search for them. It doesn't matter how far I have to go, I am determined to get my sheep back! I love my sheep. I am their shepherd. They will respond only to my voice. Oh, I know about Randall's objection to my authority. Maybe he will come to understand that I see undeveloped potential in him. And Jacqueline, ready to recruit alpacas—she has a good mind, but she is too concerned with herself.

My sheep are starving. Even with the good pasture before them, they have eaten what tantalizes but does not nourish. They have been full, but they need to be fed. It saddens me that they aren't always eager to graze in the good pasture. That is why their lives depend on me.

Michele, the shepherd, whose name means "one who is like God," is an appealing shepherd. Her mix of love and authority, zeal for her flock and tenderness, and judgment and grace are all found in Ezekiel 34:

For thus says the Sovereign [or Lord] God: I, I myself will search for my sheep, and will seek them out. As a shepherd seeks out the flock when some of the sheep have been scattered abroad, so will I seek out my sheep; and I will rescue them from all places where they have been scattered on a day of cloud and thick shadow. And I will bring them out from the peoples, and gather them from the countries, and will bring them into their own land; and I will feed them on the mountains of Israel, by the fountains, and in all the inhabited places of the country. I will feed them with good pasture, and upon the mountain heights of Israel shall be their pasture; there they shall lie down in good grazing land, and on fat pasture they shall feed on the mountains of Israel. I myself will be the shepherd of my sheep, and I will make them lie down, says the Sovereign [*or* Lord] God. I will seek the lost, and I will bring back the strayed, and I will bind up those who are crippled, and I will strengthen those who are weak, and the fat and the strong I will watch over; I will feed them in justice.

Therefore, thus says the Sovereign [*or* Lord] God to them: I, I myself will judge between the fat sheep and the lean sheep. Because you push with side and shoulder, and thrust at all the weak with your horns, till you have scattered them abroad, I will save my flock, they shall no longer be a prey; and I will judge between sheep and sheep. . . . I, the Sovereign [*or* Lord], have spoken. (Ezek. 34:11-16, 20-22, 24*b* ILL)

As you listened to the sheep, did anything catch your attention, sounding familiar in the ways they expressed themselves or in their attitudes? Perhaps you are like Randall, who gets angry and bridles against any authority that tries to direct your action or to change your self-destructive behavior. For Randall, all the problems are outside himself. He is never at fault, and what others do is open for criticism. Completely unable to put himself inside the wool of other sheep or in the shoes of the shepherd, he experiences strong emotions with no thought for the equally important feelings of others. His name (see note below) is expressive of one who maintains distance between self and others by aggressive behavior and a stance that assigns fault to everyone else. Few of us desire to see the self-destructiveness within ourselves. It is always someone else's fault: "They're coming down on me too hard! I know what's good for me, and besides it's my life. Let me live it the way I want!" But life is lived in relationships, and when we are determined to go our own way, relationships are shattered or painfully die.

Jacqueline is lost in her own little world. She is unable to give or to share in the joys of others, to extend herself to others, or to see the mutuality of giving and receiving. This is a lonely place to be.

Then there are persons like Miriam, who make a profession out of manipulation. Their smiles and sheep's eyes are ready. They appear to be obedient and cooperative, but it is all feigned for the purpose of achieving their own goals and ends. Harder to spot, this way of behaving is quite insidious. With a name that means "rebellion," this covert insolence is cancerous for the "Miriams."

Humility is not the most popular quality in our world, which celebrates corporate take-overs, raw power, and "Rambo" movies. We think that if we were in charge everything would be different. Or we have the illusion that we are in control and that everyone must obey our every command. As long as we believe that we are the authors of power, our lives will be on a dead end road.

I invite you to begin or to continue a journey of self-awareness, a journey that requires honesty, desire for change, and a willingness to look deep within. At first the load you will carry will be heavy, but as you proceed (even with the inevitable regressions), your load will become lighter. Self-deception is burdensome; honesty gives buoyancy.

We can journey together in the Spirit of God. Most of the sheep are not ready—Randall blames; Jacqueline has formed a world around her own wishes; Miriam fakes life. They have tried to take charge of lives that are vacant attempts at living.

Stephen perceives and admits his absolute dependence on

the shepherd. He acknowledges his conceit of self-reliance. Between our sinfulness and God's grace is less of a chasm and more of a breath: "God, I have sinned."

NOTE

1. The names of the sheep and the shepherd were chosen for their meanings as found in Webster's *New World Dictionary of the American Language,* 2nd College Edition (New York: Simon and Schuster, 1982). *Michele,* the feminine form of *Michael,* means "one like God." *Randall* is a combination of the Anglo-Saxon word *rand* ("shield") and the Old Norse *wulf* ("wolf"). *Jacqueline* is the feminine form of Jack or Jacob and means "supplanter." *Miriam* (a variant of Mary) means "rebellion." *Stephen* means "crown."

In chapter 4, there is an affirmation that God is. Only through God who is a greater power than we are, can we become whole.

> *Every round goes higher, higher;*
> *Every round goes higher, higher,*
> *Every round goes higher, higher;*
> *Soldiers of the cross.*

FOUR

UNDER AUTHORITY

I cannot cease what I never began, relinquish what I have never had.

Prison choirs are noted for the music they produce. They also have a reputation among prison staffs for being potential sources of cacophony, not harmony. Seedbeds for power struggles, inmate directors and inmate officers can come and go on a rapid basis when their authority is questioned by other inmates. The result can be mutiny among the singers.

As a prison chaplain, I have witnessed and have been in the middle of stormy times for choirs. One day an inmate director came to me. "Last night's rehearsal was a mess," she stated with vigor. "Some of the women weren't giving their best; others were talking. I told them that they should either get with it or not be in the choir. Then the choir president spoke up. She said that I didn't have the right to say those things, that it wasn't my job. When the fuss continued, the president said that she would disband the present choir and go back to the original members." Then came the unexpected request: "May we change our name and sing at the chapel service tomorrow night?"

"Remember," I replied, "you do rehearse in the chapel and sing for services, but I have no authority to let you do what you are asking because you are not sponsored by the chapel staff.

But I doubt that one or two people from the group can dissolve the entire group."

I encouraged her to have the choir or a smaller group, representing both sides, work jointly on a solution. "You need to face the issues that have been raised," I concluded.

When a meeting was called for 10:00 the next night, a key figure in the struggle for dominance said, "I will probably be asleep!" Absence was one weapon in a large arsenal. It became increasingly apparent that instead of singing for the Lord, the goal of some in the group was power and control.

The following day, three inmates, including the director, were waiting for me—the battle was still raging. Again I urged them to work out their differences. I advised them that the way one speaks to someone sets the tone for future communication. To two of the inmates, I tried to give food for thought: "You probably have noticed that I can be strong-willed and intent on my own goals. I see some of the same characteristics in you. Cooperation for the common good often means giving up individual desires." As an afterthought, to affirm a less domineering example of leadership, I turned to Carolyn,[1] the assistant director, and said, "But you aren't so strong-willed."

I hoped the advice about tone of voice would bear fruit, although, I admit, it didn't deal with the root of the controversy. I was surprised that my comment to Carolyn had the greater impact. Later, she came to me, concerned about what I had said. Her gentle demeanor had not been without price. "For twenty-two years I was abused by my husband. I tried to get away, and he threatened to kill me. When I would get the courage to leave, he always found me. One night after I was separated from my husband, I got into an argument with an acquaintance. It wasn't over anything important, but suddenly he grabbed me around the neck. All I could think about was that I didn't want to get beaten again. I shot him. I didn't mean to do it, but I did!"

In the story of the choir and Carolyn's disclosure—with scars still very apparent—there is a clear problem, and there are questions about authority: Who has authority to take action?

On what is the authority based? Who will be the person(s) under the authority?

Ephesians 5:21 begins: "Be subject to one another. . . . " Why should one be subject to another? Because one is the wife and the other the husband? Because one is an inmate and another an officer? Because one is the boss, the other the employee; one the parent, the other the child? Position, financial status, sex, and age are not to be indicators of how to treat others. One should be subject to another "out of reverence for Christ."

A child always questions authority in the household, and by the time the child is two years old, battle lines can be drawn and a contest of wills can develop between the parents and the child. In such a situation, one could expect to hear the child described with the degrading term "terrible twos." One of the most important maturational tasks for a child at this age may be at risk: to be able to assert oneself, thereby developing an identity distinguished from others. When the child says no, that child is separating self and learning how to exert authority and individuality. If a child can't say no at home and be respected for making that decision, how can that child as a teenager say no to peers who would entice him or her with drugs, alcohol, cigarettes, or sexual promiscuity?

When I taught English as a foreign language in Germany, the students were responsive to my democratic style. They were noisy at times, but they did learn English. Most classes were going well, with one exception. Each day the fourteen- and fifteen-year-olds and I had a battle over who was in charge, and I rarely was the one chosen! I became more and more distressed about the fact that few of the intended goals for learning a language were being reached.

Finally I spoke to their homeroom teacher. He was baffled by my lack of control. He thought that the best way for him to offer a solution to the problem was to observe the class. He did, and I was shocked! I had prepared more than we could possibly cover in a typical day's class, and we zipped right through it. I panicked and was embarrassed by my limited plans, with my having to wing it for twenty very long minutes. What made the difference that day? In the presence of the other, more autocratic, teacher, the students were on their best behavior, almost in military demeanor. Everyone sat erect in his or her chair, answered questions, and contributed on cue. You could have heard a pin drop between responses.

"What seems to be the difficulty, Frau Johns?" the other teacher asked me after class. I mumbled something about their being better than usual, hoping to be finished with the issue. As frustrating as our previous sessions had been, I wanted no class ever again to be so totally inert and routine, without enthusiasm or energy. That rambunctious, boisterous crew needed to learn how to manage themselves, not to be coerced into obedience. Totalitarianism teaches subservience and acquiescence, and it is a breeding ground for rebellion, not for learning to submit willingly to a trustworthy authority.

One comment I shall forever cherish was from the parish priest who taught religion classes in the same school. His observation of the impact of allowing expression while teaching self-control enabled me to balance the picture. "I always like to follow your teaching," he said. "The students are easier to work with, not so riled up like they've been in a cage. You must be a good teacher." These were heartening words to a discouraged, but still hopeful, teacher.

It is one set of circumstances and one sense of self when I am subservient without a conscious choice. When I intentionally put myself under the authority of others, who are under the authority of Christ, there can be mutual respect and trust that they will abuse the power inherent in their roles.

One of the most demanding places to balance the nuances of authority is within marriage. How does this advice sound to you: "Husbands, obey your wives. Because the wife is ruler of the husband. Let husbands bow down to their wives in all things." This may sound familiar, and it may be startling, but you have read my retelling accurately. This advice is based on Ephesians 5, and in it a predictable order of authority has been reversed.

If you had lived in first-century Ephesus, you would have been equally surprised—if not shocked—at Paul's counsel about marriage and the relation of the wife to the husband. John Temple Bristow, in his book *What Paul Really Said About Women,* says that Greek philosophy and Jewish custom of the time of Paul (and well before) were for women to be under the authority of men, passing from the custodian father to the custodian husband.[2]   But in Ephesians 5, the heaviest load in the marriage is on the husband. The husband is instructed to *love* the wife. The love being called for is self-denying, self-sacrificing. It is the same kind of love that Christ has for the church. I don't think many wives would have a problem being under an authority that is an unconditional love. Wives would know that any decision, any action, would be made out of that kind of an understanding of the relationship.

> Be filled with the Spirit, addressing one another in psalms and hymns and spiritual songs, singing and making melody to the Sovereign [*or* Lord] with all your heart, always and for everything giving thanks to God the Father [*and Mother*] in the name of our Sovereign [*or* Lord] Jesus Christ.
> Be subject to one another out of reverence for Christ, wives to your husbands as to the Sovereign [*or* Lord]. For the husband is the head of the wife as Christ is the head of the church, the body of Christ, of which Christ is Savior. In the same way that the church is subject to Christ in everything, so are wives to husbands. Husbands, love your wives, as Christ loved the church and gave up Christ's self on its behalf, so as to sanctify the church, having cleansed it by the washing of water with the word, in order to present it to Christ in splendor, without spot or wrinkle or any such thing, that the church might be holy and without blemish. (Eph. 5:18*b*-27 ILL)

These verses are analogies: Christ and the church are analogous to the wife and the husband.

Are these words binding today? When female and male are paired, questions arise: Are there genetic traits that are unique to either sex? How does the hidden curriculum of our culture define the roles of wife and husband? Do men have intellectual superiority over women or vice versa? I aver that the question is spiritual, not relating to sex. It is the fundamental question of who is going to try to control our lives, or to what allegiances we will give ourselves. We'd best give ourselves away with great care, for all but God will exact penalties, and these will be too dear. Going against God's laws and authority produces pain and involuntary servitude.

I believe that the essential message in the passage from Ephesians is that Christ is the authority over the church. The writer has based his thought on a relationship all the readers would know, either by experience or by observation: marriage. Although the female-male description is culturally bound— that is, the authority of the father/husband over the daughter/ wife—a complete study of the passage reveals a significant departure from the attitudes of that day, although that is hard to discern with twentieth-century eyes and the limitations of translations.

The church is, of course, us—persons participating in the life of the organized church. The writer of Ephesians wants us to be subject to Christ. Christ is the head, not in an intellectual sense, but as the authority. Jesus said to his disciples, "All authority in heaven and on earth has been given to me" (Matt. 28:18 RSV). Authority has to have a source, and for Christ that is God.

Carolyn's husband thought that he had the right to abuse his wife and their children. That is not the kind of authority that is explained in Ephesians. That is domination and cruelty under the guise of a husband's "rights."

The prison choir director hoped she had the authority to rename the choir and to let that group sing in the service. The central way Christ had for showing his great love was by dying to his own physical self. There seemed to be little effort on the part of persons in the choir to let their own self-centered needs die so that the choir as a whole might become an instrument for ministry through music. We become as adulterers when we have authorities in our lives other than Christ. In *A Gift for God,* Mother Teresa has expressed what our being subject to

Christ would look and be like: "Put yourself completely under the influence of Jesus, so that he may think his thoughts in your mind, do his work through your hands, for you will be all-powerful with him to strengthen you."[3]

A special relationship—yes, a mystical relationship— is offered to us as the body of Christ, the church. Being the church means giving up—or not taking on—authorities of this world. Attempts to serve two authorities are not uncommon, but neither is satisfied with the other, and internal conflict is ever-present.

When we turn our entire lives over to the authority of God in Christ, our lives—which had been drifting, chaotic, or unmanageable—have God as the compass. Then we have direction as we move around that which gives coherence and sanity to our lives.

We are offered the sure, unfailing power and authority of God, whose love for us is mystical and self-giving. Will you give God power over your life? Will you accept God's authority?

NOTES

1. Carolyn is not the inmate's real name.

2. John Temple Bristow, *What Paul Really Said About Women* (San Francisco: Harper & Row, 1988), p. 39.

3. Mother Teresa of Calcutta, *A Gift for God: Prayers and Meditations* (San Francisco: Harper & Row, 1975), p. 37.

Bringing together steps 3 through 7 includes an examination of conscience and confession to God, self, and others of particular defects of character and petition to God to change these shortcomings.

FIVE

WAITING FOR THE LIGHT TO SHINE

I had heard that the Rabbi from Nazareth was in town. I wanted very badly to meet him; yet, I wanted no part of him. You see, I was weary of the sinful life I had lived, but I was afraid of leaving the familiar for a fresh start. What if I failed? What would my friends say? Would I lose those people with whom I was comfortable if I went to see Jesus?

I found out that the Rabbi was to have dinner at the home of Simon the Pharisee. As I approached Simon's house, my courage failed. Simon was a good man; everyone knew that. There was as much difference between us as the difference between cold and hot. He was brought up in the synagogue. He knew all the laws and faithfully obeyed them. By even entering his house, I would make him unclean. Simon would not be glad to see me. But I had come that far, with the flask of ointment I was clutching reminded me of my earlier resolve. A stirring deep within me directed my reluctant feet onward.

I entered the room and saw Jesus talking and laughing with the other guests. I went around behind him, not daring to look him straight in the eye. I placed the flask on the floor. Then I felt quite foolish—I had made no provision for water to bathe his dusty feet. Yet, my gracious God provided. Once I was near Jesus, all those years of misdeeds, pain, and sorrow flowed from me in a rush. It was with my salty tears that I washed his feet, and with my hair I dried them. Then I kissed his feet and softened them with oil. The scent rose pleasantly around me.

Jesus seemed not to notice me. Then I heard what filled me with purest joy: "Your sins are forgiven," Jesus said to me. Incredibly, the weight of years of wrongdoing was washed away from me. I felt light and beautiful. I was clean. Then Jesus said, "Your faith has saved you. Go, in peace." I picked up the empty bottle and without a word left Simon's house.

Later, I heard that Simon was furious with me. He had come very close to having me thrown out of his house. They say he was mumbling something about if Jesus were a prophet, he would have known how sinful I was and would not have let me touch him. I am glad I didn't hear it at the time!

The riddle Jesus posed to Simon in response to his anger is one that I understand quite well after that night. "Simon," Jesus said, "Suppose someone is owed $500 from one person and $50 from another, neither of whom can pay the loan back. If the lender forgives them both their debts, which borrower do you think will love the lender more?"

"The one who was forgiven the greater debt," Simon replied.

"You are absolutely correct, Simon," Jesus responded (see Luke 7:39-43).

Then they say the Rabbi started talking about me. Jesus hadn't seemed to take note of what I was doing at all. He spoke about how I had taken care of him, when Simon, the host, had totally neglected his responsibility of washing the dust and dirt of the streets from the feet of his guest. He told them that my sins were many (and I can assure you, Jesus knew me and my sins!), but they were forgiven because I had demonstrated such great love. I am not certain what I expected to happen that evening, but not in my wildest imagination could I have expected a life wiped clean from sin.

All this was going on while I was there, but I was so absorbed in the public nature of my confession that I heard only when Jesus spoke directly to me. "Your sins are forgiven. Your faith has made that possible. In peace, you may leave this house."

I don't have to tell you that I haven't been the same since that evening. Things have not been perfect for me. Some scoff at my new life, looking for and pointing out the times I fall, make mistakes, or get weary and do nothing. Some persons whom I thought were my friends are no longer my friends. But Jesus knows and understands how hard it is for me not to go back to my sinful habits. He forgave me then; he forgives me still. In that assurance, I experience shalom.

Some surprising similarities and stark contrasts between the sinful woman and Huckleberry Finn, a likeable character created by Mark Twain, are worth examining. In the book *The Adventures of Huckleberry Finn,* Huck never settles the tug-of-war between his innate goodness and the moral dictates of his town. Townspeople bombard him with advice on how to avoid hell, and he doesn't take to it too kindly. An unexpected streak of decency stirs in Huck when the slave Jim escapes and is then recaptured. Although Huck's religious training causes him to believe that his helping Jim will send him somewhere besides heaven, he declares that he will "steal Jim out of slavery again."

In the action the forgiven woman took, and to some degree in Huck's life, we can discern Steps 3 through 7 of the Alcoholics Anonymous 12 Steps program. Step 3 says that we must decide to turn our lives over to God's care, or to our "higher power."

By finding out where Jesus was and going to him, the woman made a conscious decision to turn her life and will over to God. Because Huck's upbringing by an alcoholic father and the civilizing attempts by the widow Watson and others in the town were at odds with each other, Huck's primary understanding of God is that of an avenger. Huck says that Providence has gotten his attention by "slapping me in the face and letting me know my wickedness was being watched all the time from up there in heaven." A combination of love for Jim and love of adventure propels Huck to freeing Jim after his capture. Our twentieth-century morality applauds Huck's action and would say to him that rather than going against the will of God, he had done precisely what God wanted him to do. But Huck senses no affirmation from God for his actions.

Huck goes through intense soul-searching, which is AA's step 4, in his moral inventory. Unfortunately, Huck's efforts run aground. He tries to pray, but he cannot articulate a prayer. He assesses the reason for his failure as his involvement in assisting Jim in obtaining his freedom. Actually, he was unable to pray because his God-given conscience had been numbed by a life of lies—the best way he knew to survive.

The woman in the story from Luke is more successful. I can imagine her thinking about and remembering what she had done in the past. I can imagine that she didn't deal with everything. Perhaps all her sins did not come to mind because she had no perception yet of the ungodly nature of her actions, or maybe she pushed down thoughts of some of her misdeeds. But she had sufficiently inventoried herself to be aware and ready to admit that she had sinned.

For Step 5, as well, Huck is found wanting. That step requires an exact admission of wrongs. This should be done to ourselves, to another person, and to God. Huck reviews his life and finds it to be lacking morally, but he assigns blame to those who have taught him and to his precarious home life. So his inventory lacks his acknowledgment of his weakness and culpability. The story in Luke reveals no words spoken by the woman, but her act of contrition in a public arena was a confessional shout to others: "I have come before you, and you know I have been worldly. I am sorry for my wrong deeds."

By being penitent and expressing our sorrow, we can demonstrate our contrition when we have hurt others. The confession may be as simple as saying "I am sorry. I was wrong." If the guilt is real and the confession genuine, we will experience release and relief afterwards. The actual concession to another person of wrongs committed has a therapeutic power.

A recovering addict once told me that she had confessed her wrongs thousands of times, but she had not known how to go further. Finally she articulated the realization: "I wasn't God, and I needed help!" For her, that meant making her public confession a vital part of the process of healing. She did this in her AA group. In that act of humility, in the open and specific acceptance of her misdeeds, the burden of her guilt was lifted. She also discovered that her pain was not unique, so the exchange of hurt made the group a community, supporting one another. Step 5 is not one to gloss over details, because it makes us face "the exact nature of our wrongs."

Steps 6 and 7 take us to the point of giving up our willfulness as we petition God to remove our character defects. We can surmise that the woman was prepared to give up her character defects. Because Huck doesn't recognize his personal defects, this action is unthinkable for him. After lying his way in and out (mostly in) of innumerable tight spots, it is a miracle that he still knows the truth. Huck's forced independence, by virtue of having no real family, and his clearly articulated individualism are both high walls that are not easily torn down in order for him to become responsible to others.

It is one thing for us to admit that we have sinned. It is another for us to be willing to make changes. I have heard people say that they have done wrong, and I have said that I have done wrong. But I and others do not automatically correct the attitudes and behavior that caused the fault. Without the conscious change, the confession is window dressing and possibly self-pity.

Persons addicted to drugs or alcohol develop giant egos as defense strategies. But any one of us can have an inflated ego. The addict I quoted earlier said that when she brought herself down to being a sinner, then God could deal with her. It is a measure of faith to admit that we are not self-sufficient. And it is a measure of faith to admit that God is able to remove from us the harmful thoughts that shape our attitudes and the resulting attitudes that impel us into actions that are hurtful to others, to God, and to ourselves.

What a wonderful experience it is to be forgiven! But even though it can be an exhilarating experience, it is not to be sought as a "high" to substitute for the destructive highs in life.[1]

When we overcome our pride and put God first, our lives take on a peacefulness and holiness that were otherwise unattainable.

Perhaps you tend to be like the sinful, forgiven woman—with her years of transgressions (the kind so easily spotted by pharisaism)—or like Huck—whose inherent goodness inspires him to do justice, but whose clouded thinking and way of living engender the "self-made man" mentality that may make him incapable of accepting correction. But many of us are like the good man Simon. Externally correct, proper in religious duties, we can be insensitive, critical, unforgiving, and too wrapped up in ourselves to enjoy godly people, like the woman forgiven by Christ.

We borrow trouble. We anticipate pain and hurt. It never ceases to amaze me that when I confess my fault to God and to others, the pain is a bit less than when I stupidly hang onto my pride. It is imperative that we examine our conscience; that we confess to God, to ourselves, and to others our particular weakness in character; and that we pray for God's removal of those defects. When that is done, our spiritual journey has not been interrupted, but is proceeding well.

Our journey is out; our journey is in. On the journey, we meet God and discover God within. It is a journey to find that our lives and our God are intricately and superbly connected. It is a journey made with earthly companions. And as we journey, we recognize and name our shortcomings, extending ourselves as we take steps toward restoring broken bonds.

Huck Finn made it to Broadway in the musical *Big River*. One song sung by Huck describes his long years in darkness. From the first slow rendition of "Waitin' for the Light to Shine" to the energetic reprise, Huck's lack of moral and spiritual core is described as one who has waited and waited for the light to shine. The darkness has been deep and unending. Isaiah says, "the people who walked in darkness have seen a great light" (9:2*a*).

The sinful woman and the misdirected Huck saw the greatest of lights. Huck was—even in his ethically correct decision—still lost. The woman embraced the light. We need not wait for the light to shine, for the dark has been split by an eternal radiance.

NOTE

1. Because addicts may substitute one addictive substance for another—and in denial pronounce themselves cured—it is a serious mistake to borrow language like "high" and "fix" when speaking of religious experience. There are persons who are addicted to religion! (See chapter 9, "Radical Religion.")

SIX

IT IS BETTER FOR ME TO DIE!

Whom do you dislike intensely? Perhaps you come close to hating that person. If you are thinking of someone, you can imagine that you would avoid this person at all times. Perhaps hearing someone's name can raise your blood pressure. Whom can you simply not tolerate?

Now, clearly imagine that person. Imagine that what happens next is that you receive a directive from God: "Go to your adversary, the person you detest, and tell that person that because of his or her great wickedness, that person will die in three weeks."

Your first response upon receiving this command may be overwhelming joy at your enemy's punishment. Finally, you think, my enemy is going to get what is due! But a second thought comes. Maybe this isn't too hot an assignment after all. You really don't want to have anything at all to do with your foe, and what if the person decides to reform? You know God pretty well, and you know that if the person repents, there is no telling how merciful God could decide to get. No, you conclude, that message was not from God; maybe the wires got crossed up in the transmission. It was from the devil, and you have no intention of fulfilling it. So you do everything to avoid contact with or thinking about your nemesis. This works for a few days, but it becomes obvious that God is quite serious and makes your duty crystal clear: "I'm talking to you, and I expect you to do as I say." One clue is when people start asking you about the assignment from God and you haven't even mentioned it to anyone.

Reluctantly, you go to the person. And wonder of wonders, the person gets the message, is quite sobered by it, starts fasting, and turns the profligate life 180 degrees around: a true *metanoia*! You don't have to be a college graduate to figure out the next part of the scenario: God is so excited about the conversion that God cancels the whole plan of destruction.

That makes you really mad! You didn't want to go to that person anyway, and you figured that God would probably go soft on the deal. You are standing there, looking the fool, while your enemy is safe in the loving, forgiving arms of God. That is not justice! You are so angry that you tell God about your feelings: "Just go ahead and kill me now, God. It certainly is better to die than to live with this humiliation!"

An engaging Old Testament character, Jonah, should get together with you. You could talk about tough times, crying on each other's shoulders. Jonah had a similar experience.

> Then the word of the Lord came to Jonah the second time, saying, "Arise, go to Nineveh, that great city, and proclaim to it the message that I tell you." So Jonah arose and went to Nineveh, according to the word of the Lord. Now Nineveh was an exceedingly great city, three days' journey in breadth. Jonah began to go into the city, going a day's journey. And he cried, "Yet forty days, and Nineveh shall be overthrown!" And the people of Nineveh believed God; they proclaimed a fast, and put on sackcloth, from the greatest of them to the least of them. . . .
>
> When God saw what they did, how they turned from their evil way, God repented of the evil which he had said he would do to them; and he did not do it. . . .
>
> But it displeased Jonah exceedingly, and he was angry. And he prayed to the Lord and said, "I pray thee, Lord, is not this what I said when I was yet in my country? That is why I made haste to flee to Tarshish; for I knew that thou art a gracious God and merciful, slow to anger, and abounding in steadfast love,

and repentest of evil. Therefore now, O Lord, take my life from me, I beseech thee, for it is better for me to die than to live." (Jon. 3:1-5, 10; 4:1-3 RSV)

Maybe you can empathize with Jonah, remembering how you would have felt under similar circumstances.

Jonah did get a rough assignment. Nineveh was an Assyrian city, an enemy of the Hebrews. Why would anyone go to the land of an enemy and speak of God? And what possible concern could God have for those people? After all, the Assyrians weren't the chosen people!

Jonah tried to trick God by getting on a ship sailing west. It seems, however, that God's sphere extended beyond Jonah's hallowed land. God caused a mighty storm at sea that scared everybody on the ship—everyone, that is, but Jonah, who was relaxed enough to be asleep. Before the storm was over, however, Jonah did some testifying. He realized that the storm was caused by his disobedience, and he started talking about self-destruction, asking to be thrown into the sea. The sailors unhappily comply with Jonah's request by throwing him overboard. When the sea ceased raging, the mariners made sacrifice and vows to God, so awed were they by the power of God (Jon. 1:4-16).

I venture to guess that Jonah thought that was curtains for him, and maybe he was relieved. But we can imagine the "worst case scenario," and that is what happened: A big fish swam by and swallowed him. Jonah's poetic ability emerges after having time to get perspective on his situation from the belly of the fish:

> When I felt my life slipping away,
>   then, O Lord, I prayed to you,
>   and in your holy Temple you heard me.
> Those who worship worthless idols
>   have abandoned their loyalty to you.
> But I will sing praises to you;
>   I will offer you a sacrifice
>   and do what I have promised.
> Salvation comes from the Lord!
> (Jon. 2:7-9 GNB)

It sounds to me like Jonah was whistling in the dark. It must have done the trick, because shortly thereafter Jonah made it to Nineveh, dry and in a miserable frame of mind.

After Jonah's persuasive prophesying, the king of Nineveh took no chances and declared that not only should the people fast and be covered with sackcloth, but the same should be true of the animals as well. That must have been quite a sight to see. Food prices probably dropped when everybody and everything quit eating. Jonah was an overnight success! But talk about hard to please—Jonah was still one unhappy man, and he moaned to God: "Do me in, if you don't mind. It's better for me to die." With the same love that characterized God's initial concern and then forgiveness of the people of Nineveh, God spoke to Jonah, "Is your anger at me justified?"

Jonah sensed that he was not getting through to God, so Jonah went outside the city wall and built a shelter to wait in "till he should see what would become of the city" (Jon. 4:5). God made a plant grow up over Jonah, to shade him from the heat. Jonah was glad to have the plant over him, but he should have checked with a local botanist, because that plant, the castor oil plant, was delectable to a native worm. Soon the plant provided no more shade. No shade and the stifling hot wind (both arranged by God), caused Jonah to be near fainting, but he had enough breath to grouse again, "It is better for me to die than to live."

God's patience was wearing thin, but God tried again to get through to Jonah: "What is your problem, man?"

"Just finish me off, please!" Jonah wailed.

"Get your priorities straight!" God reproved Jonah. "You are moaning over the plant, which is not of your own making, and you are totally ignoring the fact that more than 120,000 lives have been spared! You are wound up in your own personal loss, while all those people in Nineveh are desperate for direction in their lives. I care about them! Have a heart, Jonah!"

Jonah was absorbed in his own desires. If something didn't fit his goals, he made no effort to invest himself in it. Jonah didn't invite others into his life. Rather than opening himself up to the people of Nineveh—sharing their fears of imminent destruction or rejoicing in the miraculous reversal of the prophetic preaching—he withdrew from them.

During World War II, POWs, in defiance of international agreement, were forced by their captors to build a railroad through the jungles of Thailand. Disease was rampant. Starvation was the menu, and the physical exhaustion was profound. In that atmosphere, selfishness was king; walls were built out of blocks of fear. When there seemed to be nothing for which to live, survival became an obsession. Out of this pathetic human state emerged "The Ladder Club," of which Ernest Gordon says: "the weak were trampled underfoot, the sick ignored or resented, the dead forgotten." The motto made clear the terms, "I've got the ladder . . . I'm all right."[1]

Then a change began to take place. A gradual blowing of the Spirit began to bring a new atmosphere. It came after some of the POWs began to study Scripture, which led them to a radical living out of forgiveness—of one another and of their enemy. Although the external circumstances remained—and it is certain that not all of the thousands of POWs in the camp began to understand and to reform from the insidious and spiritually devastating effect of "The Ladder Club"—the ladder was being dismantled as God's word fed the starving.

Jonah was in a foreign land, the land of his country's adversaries, as were the POWs. Jonah was asked to do good to those who had abused his homeland, as were the POWs. However, Jonah had to contend with nothing like the trauma the POWs faced. In contrast to some in the forced labor camp in Thailand, Jonah would not forgive the people of Nineveh, and he would not forgive God.

Haven't we all been distressed when something good came to someone we thought deserved the opposite? Doesn't it feel good occasionally to reproach a sinner and to see the sinner squirm under our indictment? An honest response would be yes. Like Jonah, while we give lip-service to proclaiming God's

word, secretly we hope it doesn't take and that the scoundrel
will get what is richly deserved—in our assessment!

When that is our predicament, the only correct response is to
confess our hostility and to petition God to change our secret
desire. Just as we want God's mercy and grace to extend to us,
so also we need to remember that God loves our enemies, who
are of equal value, exactly as God loves us. That sounds great,
but it is hard to take to heart.

I would like to think that Jonah finally got God's message to
quit licking his own tiny wounds of injured pride, reputation,
and misplaced nationalism. God wanted Jonah to rejoice over
the sparing of over 120,000 individuals because they had turned
from their sin, ceasing their violence.

If he did understand what God was telling him, then Jonah
would say, "I repent in dust and ashes. You are absolutely
right, God, I have been a loathsome, petty creature. Spread
some of that grace my way, because I need it." That is the
ending to the story we prefer.

Stopping where it does, the narrative has a shock effect on its
readers. A neat little "and they lived happily ever after" would
send us on to the next story with hardly a second thought.
Instead, the story invites us to put ourselves into the narrative.
Obviously, the most natural character for us to identify with is
Jonah. It is not easy to sit under the broiling sun and rejoice
over the good fortune of an enemy—but, then, if Jonah had
been celebrating with the people of Nineveh, he wouldn't have
been in the heat! We also have at least 120,000 other people
with whom to identify.

Nursing our self-righteousness, which can easily be based on
fact and prior behavior of others but not on compassion, we
become ill from our own making. God pleads with us to discard
the thermometer that is measuring our degree of discomfort.
Better still, maybe our enemy needs a turn at diagnosing us.
When we stop our pouting, we can attain enough objectivity to
envision the whole scene. Then it doesn't matter who is right
and who is wrong. The great God Almighty repented! If God

can take a second look and change, can we not also? If we put our priorities in order, we will understand better the forgiving nature of God, which is extended to all: enemy, friend, or self.

Watch out for the Jonah in yourself. It can get lonely sitting under a withered castor oil plant in the hot sun, wishing all the while that you were the only one to receive God's grace. It definitely gives you less time to know and to enjoy God. I doubt that Jonah ever got his priorities lined up, but that should not stop us from doing so! "Ladder Club" members pay high dues. Will Jonah be our mirror image, or the antithesis of who we can be as we invite God to remove the defects in our character?

NOTE

1. Ernest Gordon, *Through the Valley of the Kwai* (New York: Harper & Row, 1962), p. 75.

In steps 8 and 9, we are instructed to make a list of and "direct amends to" persons who have been hurt by us, wherever making amends would not cause further hurt.

SEVEN

STRAP HANGING

Hanging by a strap on a subway or bus requires a combination of tenacity and agility. With your hand securely on the strap above your head, your muscles grow weary. Legs must be firmly planted, with feet able to move swiftly to regain balance at any unexpected action of the public transportation. A shoulder-to-shoulder crowd has its advantages, the most notable one being that a lurch or quick stop throws everyone together, supporting each other.

Staying upright and on your feet is one matter—for that, a crowd comes in handy—but getting a seat is an entirely different challenge. When two people are standing for every one person sitting, your best hope is a vacancy within inches of your strap. Then it may be only quickness of movement and determination that give you the pleasure of a cushion, back rest, and relaxation. Obviously, it would be much better for everyone if there were one seat for every passenger!

A young boy growing up in Mississippi in the 1940s was the son of a sharecropper father, who died when the boy was thirteen. Soon after, the boy's mother became ill. As the eldest boy, he knew it fell to him to see that she received medical help. So he hitched up the team of mules and took her to see a doctor in the little town nearby. The doctor said that she needed to go to Hattiesburg for the necessary treatment, and that meant riding the bus. The boy and his mother went to the bus station, climbed onto the bus, and walked past empty seats to the curtain cordoning off the last few rows of seats for blacks. Behind the curtain, no empty seats were left. They spent the hour-long ride hanging by straps, the mother growing sicker and sicker. The young boy became very angry as he looked at his mother and at the empty seats in the front of the bus—for whites only. To sit in those seats meant breaking the law, and they dared not do that!

At last in Hattiesburg, they had to walk about eight blocks, taking a further toll on the mother, weak from her illness and the exertion the trip had demanded. After waiting hours to see the doctor, she was given medication and sent on her way. Either the medication was not appropriately administered or the illness was increasing its fury. Every step of the eight blocks back to the bus was a trial as the mother's condition worsened.

They made it to the bus again, past the empty seats and back to the curtain and the full seats. As before, there was no place for them to sit. Again they hung by the straps. A young white boy, seeing the woman standing at the edge of the curtain, obviously in pain, offered her his seat, but he was restrained by a man sitting with him. The boy tried again, and again he was stopped. Tears were rolling down the mother's cheeks as the trip and the sickness became unbearable. Anger burned bright and hot in her son's heart.

By the time they got home after the long ordeal, the son resolved never to ride a bus again. He knew that he could not forget what white people had done to his mother that day.

Years later, when he was in seminary, he got news of the death of an aunt. His fierce resolve not to ride a bus had remained unbroken. He flew from Atlanta to New Orleans. Then he faced the awful truth: unless he rode a bus, he would not make it to his aunt's funeral on time. Taking the first step toward a decision, he grudgingly got a cab to the bus station. There, to his surprise, he saw not two waiting rooms—one for the coloreds and one for the whites—but one spacious and attractive waiting room for everyone. There was no shortage of seats.

Loading the bags onto the bus was a black man, looking fine in his uniform. Expecting a white driver, the young man was amazed to see the uniformed man mount the steps and take his place behind the wheel of that bus. There were no curtains on this bus, and the seminarian proudly claimed his seat directly behind the black driver! The view was extraordinary. Despite the sad purpose of his trip, the front-row passenger was feeling quite splendid.

About ten miles from his destination, the driver announced that just ahead were four passengers: three white girls and their chaperone, a nun. He said that they only had room for three, but if no one objected, he would pick up all of them and one would have to stand. The bus stopped, and the group got on. The girls were seated, and the nun took her position, hanging on a strap—right beside where the young man sat!

Suddenly the seminarian's euphoria and delight in the bus ride, his seat, and the fine driver were crushed. He watched that woman hanging on the strap, and God started talking to him. God reminded him of his years of anger, his unforgiving spirit and bitterness. The man told God that his feelings were fully justified; he had been hated and humiliated too many times to count. His mother and all his people had suffered needlessly. Back and forth they argued. Apparently God won, because the man staring at that woman no longer saw the face and clothing of a nun but instead the clothing and tear-stained face of his mother.

Without warning, and with more force than he expected, he jumped up and pointed to his vacated seat. He yelled at the woman, "Sit down!" Not knowing if she were dealing with a man for whom disobedience would further inflame the situation, she decided the best course of action was to take the seat. Standing, the young man's hand closed around the familiar strap. To his surprise, his euphoria returned, and the view was better than before. The next eight miles were the most glorious miles he ever traveled. At last his mother had a seat on the bus![1]

Paul explains how such a profound change is possible. In

Christ, the old is overcome by the new. Because God is a reconciler, the young man was able to begin the process of reconciliation between his black world and the white world of the South.

> From now on, therefore, we regard no one from a human point of view; even though we once regarded Christ from a human point of view, we regard Christ thus no longer. Therefore, if anyone is in Christ, there is a new creation; the old has passed away—the new has come.
>
> All this is from God, who through Christ reconciled us to God's self and gave us the ministry of reconciliation; that is, God was in Christ reconciling the world to God's self, not counting their trespasses against them, and entrusting to us the message of reconciliation. So we are ambassadors for Christ, God making God's appeal through us. We beseech you on behalf of Christ, be reconciled to God. (II Cor. 5:16-20 ILL)

One summer, my husband and I attended a liturgical conference in Washington, D.C. The number of participants and the structure of the conference precluded much personal interaction. The final service came, and our discomfort level rose as the Peace approached, because we were seated between two strangers, the man by my husband so large he required two seats. But as God's peace was symbolically passed from person to person, we embraced not earthly strangers, but heavenly brothers and sisters.

I have an image of Christ hugging the whole world to himself, reassuring us, loving us, smoothing out our rough edges. Another way of saying that is to look at Paul's description: "God was in Christ reconciling the world to God's self." Reconciliation means to make friendly *again,* to make consistent or bring into harmony. In reconciliation, we are restored to what we used to be before sin alienated us from God and from one another.

In the Roman Catholic Church the "Sacrament of Reconciliation" is a process from awareness of sin to change in the way we live. Whether we call that a sacrament or not, it is important that we understand the structure and the elements essential to this process. It is an act of healing, which focuses not so much on us as we try to make things right, but on God—God's action in, through, and with us. It restores us to spiritual health in God's family through a round-trip journey that brings us home again. The sinner is loved back to wholeness by God.

Dealing with our guilt specifically and concretely is the first step toward reconciliation. However, we may be misdirected from the beginning if we are dealing with an irrational guilt, instead of a rational guilt. Irrational guilt is experiencing remorse for a situation over which we had no control, but for which we are taking unnecessary blame. It is unhealthy, self-centered, self-concerned, and can become debilitating.

On the healthy side, a rational guilt signals responsibility, not making excuses (in irrational guilt, excuses are called reasons). Rational guilt leads to sorrow, then forgiveness. These are necessary for growth to holiness and wholeness.

The black man could have felt guilt for not having a team of horses to take his mother to the doctor or for not having the nerve to break the law and sit in those "white" seats. Or maybe he thought he could have worked harder, earned more money, allowing him to secure the best medical care for his mother. All that would have been irrational guilt. The rational guilt with which he finally dealt was the acknowledgment of his sin of unresolved anger, unforgiveness, and bitterness. He felt genuine sorrow, and after he knew God's judgment on him, he took the second step in reconciliation by confessing his sin to himself and to God. Although the edges were still rough, he expressed his desire for reconciliation with a hostile white world by commanding the nun to sit down. Finally his euphoria after conversion and confession became his own personal celebration—the third and final step. Rejoicing over the restored and redeemed is the fitting climax.

There was no way for him to reconcile with all the whites who had contributed to an unjust system of which the segregated seats were only a symptom. Quite unexpectedly, the nun's standing while he sat became for the man the symbolic moment for reconciliation. If it is not possible to be reconciled with the specific person toward whom we have unforgiveness, reconciliation can be accomplished through a representative of the person—sometimes without that person's knowledge.

It is not enough to experience guilt. It is not enough to offer or accept forgiveness. We aren't supposed to walk around glowing in the knowledge of God's forgiveness of us when we forgive others. As good as that is, we must not stop there. Through the third step of reconciliation, celebration, we are blessed with enthusiasm to be reconciling agents in this world. We are to be ambassadors for Christ. It is a ministry of bringing harmony, restoring the original harmony of God's creation. It is the essential purpose of our reconciliation to speak to others and to extend the reconciliation by offering it again and again. We aren't to sit back in our bus seats, as comfortable as that may be, looking out the window, soaking up the view. We need to turn our heads and see the pain of the woman or child or man hanging from the strap and get up out of our seats. It can be such joy to offer our seats to those who are barely hanging by a strap!

NOTE

1. James C. Peters, Sr., told this story from his life experience when he preached at the Alabama-West Florida Annual Conference, June 1, 1988.

EIGHT

FACE-TO-FACE

For five years Sam Keen, author and teacher of philosophy, traveled the world, collecting and studying images of how nations teach their citizens to hate their declared enemies. He discovered that there is a consistency in the metaphors. The enemy is dehumanized, and emotion-laden terms, such as *demon, barbarian, liar, mad,* and *aggressor* are used. Faces and bodies—distorted, caricatured, and made animalistic—promote hate between peoples, and a myth of "enemy" is created. Such campaigns are enormously successful, coalescing complete strangers against the fabricated notion of enemy.[1]

The documentary "Faces of the Enemy" tells of the process Sam Keen carefully followed. Keen recounts a brutal murder, committed by David Pace in 1985. Pace murdered a family of four in an acting out of his belief that there was a plan to turn the world into one communist government. Keen visited Pace in prison on several occasions and observed after a time that some of Pace's delusions were based on fragments of reality, but that Pace had believed the myth-making of the "communist as the ultimate enemy."

On one occasion, Keen expressed unexpected compassion for the offender, Pace, and the victims. The cameras captured a tragic and fragile interchange. Keen confessed to Pace: "I feel all your uncried tears and all the pain you cannot feel, but I feel for the victims more."

Pace's reply seemed unemotional: "It would have been easier if we hadn't talked."

Keen agreed. As the full weight of the internal conflict he was experiencing fell on him, he looked an enemy of society in the face and said, "Yes, it would have been easier. It is easier to remain numb. And isn't numbness the real villain?"

The process of making an enemy is a very easy one—dangerously so. The enemy can begin to take shape when we perceive that someone is coming between us and our goals. Feelings of hatred and the desire to hurt, or at least impede the person, grow. You can see it in political campaigns when dehumanizing and labeling are tactics designed to polarize and win votes. Countries count on it to advance their own cause, and leaders in government rely on it to engender support for actions that may seem outrageous to any thinking individual. Whether the enemy created is one-on-one or global, the process is irrational and thrives on stereotypes and rigid values. It causes us to think that:

> We are good. They are evil.
> We are victims. They are to blame.
> We know the truth. They lie.
> We are moral, law-abiding citizens.
> They are immoral lawbreakers.

The tabulating and polarizing are limitless, fitting whatever cause feeds our own passions.

I strongly object to the idea that enemy-making is a necessary evil to protect the interests of the nation, political party, religion, or individual. It is a contrivance seen by some as indispensable to self-preservation. There is "security and identity, but it also creates selective blindness, narrowness and rigidity because it is intrinsically conservative."[2] Rather than self-preservation, it sows the seeds of mutual obliteration. We know that from the case of David Pace, from history, and from our own lives. Pace destroyed a family, and probably he destroyed himself by the results of his delusional thinking.

It is important to visualize the scene of Pace and Keen as Keen's compassion for Pace was expressed. The two had met face-to-face. The terrible deed itself was not condoned by Keen. Pace's fantasies and emotional detachment greatly hampered congruence between the two, but Keen saw Pace's face and studied his eyes. He felt the salt of Pace's tears on his own cheeks. It is easier to remain numb, to continue our cold insensitivity, but it is against our humanity once we have seen face-to-face.

An expression of speech illustrates how we distance ourselves from persons when closeness threatens our own sense of security. When talking about persons with handicapping conditions, persons in mental hospitals, prison inmates, or anyone whose circumstance is strange to us, we are told to "treat them just like people." The word *like* is a simile, a comparing of two dissimilar things as if they were the same. So inmates, the mentally ill, and persons with handicaps are not people, but we'll talk about them as if they were. It is a matter of survival, is it not, to remain aloof from them. If these people are not our enemies, at least let's not get too close to them because they may contaminate us.

If the fear is not of contamination, it may be the anxiety of being consumed or sucked into or even sympathetic to persons whose lives are not whole and clean. The price may be too great if we let down our defenses and start caring! We don't have to be told that people's needs are great and that after we have helped one person, inevitably there will be more persons craving our assistance. It is easy to become resentful or to suffer guilt because of an overwhelming obligation to serve, especially when all attempts to assist someone are ignored.

When the awareness of needs is not equal to our energy, resentment may grow inside us. That is when we should make the effort to look at the face of the person before us, seeing Christ in that human being. When we see Christ, we feel the "uncried tears and all the pain." It is a terrible injustice to turn our faces from others because we have pigeonholed them or because the myths by which we live are intractable.

In Matthew 25, we hear the Judge decree: "If you have alleviated the hurt of these who are of least value you have done so to me." Most people who seek help are not at their best; their manner and appearance may be repellant to some. However, does God always come in attractive packaging?

The second group in the parable in Matthew 25 are the ones searching for the beautiful and whole to whom to offer their useless services. Those hungering for either real or spiritual food, are voracious. The stranger is not welcome into home or heart because his or her clothing is rumpled, dirty, or smelly. The person imprisoned as a criminal or by prisons of emotional destructiveness brings out our anxieties that the world is not as secure as we want it to be. Those righteous, white-gloved, pseudo-servants are told by the King: "You, by not receiving these little ones, have refused to help me."

How can we understand people's pain? If we are unwilling to accept the validity of someone's wounded state, we will attempt to take the place of the Judge. Psalm 27 helps us to experience the despair of rejection by describing the hopelessness felt when the most primal of relationships, that of mother and father, has been nullified. The psalmist pleads with God:

> Hear, O God . . . when I cry aloud,
> be gracious to me and answer me!
> You have said, "Seek my face."
> My heart says to you,
> "Your face, God . . . do I seek."
> Hide not your face from me.
> Turn not your servant away in anger,
> you who have been my help.
> Cast me not off, forsake me not,
> O God of my salvation!
> For my father and my mother have forsaken me,
> but God . . . will take me up.
>
> (Ps. 27:7-10 ILL)

"For my father and my mother have forsaken me. . . . " Time and again as a prison chaplain, I have heard inmates tell of parents who have abandoned them for all kinds of reasons. Perhaps the inmate has promised to change and has broken those promises. Sometimes the emotional and financial burdens are more than parents feel they can bear any longer.

One can sympathize with a parent who in exasperation proclaims that enough is enough. What is the profound pain for many inmates is the abandonment they suffered as children. Many were born to teenaged parents or to alcoholic or drug addicted parents. Many have parents who were incarcerated as well. They are shuffled here and there and often end up in situations in which there is no guarantee of security or of loving, nurturing care. The innocent may become adults who feel inadequate, who are emotional children, searching for a blood parent who is not there and will never be there. The innocent, at first a victim, may become an offender.

The curiosity we have about people who are incarcerated (and that curiosity may be morbid) was toyed with in a television program about death-row inmates. Rather than enlightening, the show deliberately obscured our seeing the humanity of the persons living on death row. The convict-mythology of our culture was promoted. Teasers promised interviews with death-row inmates. One inmate agreed to be interviewed, believing she would have the opportunity to speak to a national audience to plead with women in abusive relationships to get help to avoid the tragic outcome of her experience. Denied that time for her plea, she was painted the arch-villain.

Interview means face-to-face, and although the inmate was promised that, what was delivered were shallow questions. Superficial answers were supplied by the host when the replies were not what he wanted them to be. Millions of people saw that show, trusting that they had seen a documentary, but primarily it fed their myth of the prisoner as enemy.

Persons concerned about our justice system have become increasingly aware of the specific concerns of victims. Programs in victim-offender reconciliation have developed in the last two decades. The U. S. Association for Victim/Offender Mediation, located in Valparaiso, Indiana, exists to educate persons, to supply materials, to provide a network of similar local or state programs, and to advocate mediation.[3]

The victim and the offender are offered a face-to-face meeting, led by a trained mediator. There are rational tasks, such as the kind and amount of restitution. Questions are raised to satisfy a gnawing unsettling concern of the victim, "Why me?" The line between the factual and the emotional is not clear, because both the victim and the offender can be deeply and painfully affected by the flesh and blood reality of the other. For the first time, the offender can begin to grasp how the crime has hurt others; the numbness may be replaced by guilt and remorse. The victim may give up stereotyped images that have produced either anger or fear. No irresponsible, immoral, or illegal act is condoned. Nothing is swept under the rug, to turn into a mountain later. But forgiveness often commences in the mediation, and unseen wounds begin to heal. Bitterness is being avoided. An enemy of decency is being reformed. Victim and offender have beheld one another, human-to-human.

You may have an enemy who is not of your own creation. But no one can make you hate another in return. You can carry the image of that enemy around with you, polishing it and taking care of it. You can put it on display by telling others of the insults and injuries you have incurred from the hands of your adversary. You can protect the image by guarding incoming information, so that nothing will refute your opinion of that person. Or you can acknowledge that you have the enemy because you have nurtured the hate. You can admit that it is within your power, with God's help, to turn that around. Job went through repeated catastrophes before he comprehended this:

> I know, Lord, that you are all-powerful;
> that you can do everything you want.
> You ask how I dare question your wisdom
> when I am so very ignorant.

I talked about things I did not understand.
  about marvels too great for me to know.
You told me to listen while you spoke
  and to try to answer your questions.
In the past *I knew only what others had told me,*
  but now I have seen you with my own eyes.
So I am ashamed of all I have said
  and repent in dust and ashes.
(Job 42:2-6 GNB; italics added)

The best way to overcome an enemy is to face the person, getting to know that person as another human being. It will mean making amends and asking for forgiveness. A sense of being forsaken or abandoned can overwhelm you, if, despite opening yourself to healing through forgiving another, your adversary chooses to remain against you. But in Psalm 27, we read of comfort: "For my father and my mother have forsaken me, *but God will take me up*" (Ps. 27:10; italics added). If it's not possible or advisable for you to make amends because in so doing further hurt is caused, the process of forgiveness can begin with a spiritual counselor—priest, pastor, spiritual friend, or the Holy Spirit.

Whether we have hurt someone else or have been hurt, until we see Christ in one another and seek to restore harmony and love, we are going to continue our enemy-making, breeding violence, promoting hatred, and therein, further victimization. God does not withhold God's presence from us. Therefore, we should not withhold our humanity, even though it means risking pain, from those we have offended or who have offended us. Through the power of God's love—and that power is beyond our greatest imaginings—we can be reconciled! Seeing one another as fully human to fully human prepares us for meeting God face-to-face in our life after life.

I beseech and challenge you to shatter the destructive conceit of enemy-making, which is conceivable to the mythic mind and dangerous to the common good!

> The sacrifice acceptable to God is
>   a broken spirit;
>   a broken and contrite heart, O
>   God, thou wilt not despise.
> (Ps. 51:17 RSV)

Shattering produces brokenness, allowing us to be refashioned and made whole again by God.

NOTES

1. See Sam Keen, "The Stories We Live By," *Psychology Today* (December 1988): 43-47.

2. Ibid., p. 45.

3. Mark Umbreit, in *Crime and Reconciliation: Creative Options for Victims and Offenders* (Nashville: Abingdon Press, 1985), tells of the work of the Indiana Prisoner and Community Together (PACT) program. Alternatives to incarceration are needed not only because of the escalating cost of housing prisoners, but also for the basic purpose of effective rehabilitation, which is not always possible in a correctional institution.

In step 10, we are reminded that continued "personal inventory" and prompt admission of sin are necessary for spiritual health.

> *Seeker, do you love your Jesus?*
> *Seeker, do you love your Jesus?*
> *Seeker, do you love your Jesus?*
> *Brothers, sisters, all.*

NINE

RADICAL RELIGION

In 1967, my husband and I drove from Drew Theological School in New Jersey to Duke University in North Carolina. I was in our VW "bug" and he was in a rented van. Nine months after getting married, we were moving our worldly possessions, precious cargo to us, containing the usual assortment of clothing, appliances, and wedding presents—silver, china, and a bean bag (to throw when we had our first fight!). Near Richmond, Virginia, a tire blew on the van, flipping my husband and the van four times into a ravine separating the interstate. With a cut on his head, my husband scrambled out, getting away moments before the van and its cargo—including those wedding presents—burst into flames. In the following hours, hundreds of motorists stopped to watch the raging fire and, kindly, to offer their help.

The next day we returned to the charred ruins and picked our way through the shards of our young marriage. It was a solemn time, but we had hopes that treasures would be found—that it couldn't be as bad as it had appeared the night before. I spied in a sandy area one of our china cups. The gold rim was gleaming in the sun, and there was not a chip on it. I reached for it with jubilation. Indeed, the cup was intact, beautiful. But the handle was gone. I held it for a moment, then gently returned it to its sandy grave. Expectations diminished, my eyes vaguely surveyed the other wreckage, until I spotted the electric typewriter I used in seminary, a prized possession bought after careful budgeting. My excitement returned as I could see how well the case had survived the jolting and expulsion from the van. But the typing keys, I found after opening the case, were melted.

Jesus said to the scribes and Pharisees:

> Woe to you . . . hypocrites! for you cleanse the outside of the cup and of the plate, but inside they are full of extortion and rapacity. . . . You are like whitewashed tombs, which outwardly appear beautiful, but within they are full of dead [people's] bones and all uncleanness. So you also outwardly appear righteous to [others], but within you are full of hypocrisy and iniquity. (Matt. 23:25, 27-28)

It is distressing to think that what we see is reality, and then to discover that things are not as they appear. We have been deceived and feel like fools, which doesn't sit well. Whitewashing, feigning, pretending, or faking it—especially when it comes to religion—makes blood pressures go up!

Psychologist Gordon Allport in the 1960s gave religious superficiality a name: extrinsic religion.[1] It wasn't a new spiritual problem. The Old Testament prophets recognized religiosity and railed against it. Amos tells us how a person behaves whose whitewashed religion shifts the attention of the worshiper from justice to empty sacrifice.

> The Lord says, "I hate your religious festivals; I cannot stand them! When you bring me burnt offerings and grain offerings, I will not accept them; I will not accept the animals you have fattened to bring me as offerings. Stop your noisy songs; I do not want to listen to your harps. Instead, let justice flow like a stream, and righteousness like a river that never goes dry." (Amos 5:21-24 GNB)

This is religiosity concerned not with justice or love, but with *technique*.

Jesus referred to people who practiced extrinsic religion as hypocrites. Nineteen centuries later, humankind was still

whitewashing, and it was named "official Christianity" by
Danish philosopher and theologian Sören Kierkegaard. Extrinsic religion is alluring and rewarding in the short run; there
is a smattering of discipline and restraint. But, no rudimentary
change has been made in the life of the individual.

The race, gender, and church affiliation of the official
Christian are all irrelevant. Height, weight, nationality, and
age will give no clues to the authenticity of a person's faith. But
describing the split between thinking and action of official
Christians is enlightening. These hypocrites look for things to
work to self-advantage, with minimal inventory of self. They
are convinced that salvation is attained through their own
instigation and will. Talking about how saved they are is a
well-worn subject. The salvation they have found inherently
sets them apart, giving them special insight and judgment into
the religious commitment of everyone else.

"Good" church members, they often serve on committees
because their piety is impressive, but they are very clear on all
issues: yes or no, up or down, right or wrong. Nothing is
debatable or worth examining to discern nuances. But don't
expect the prayer meetings, Bible studies, Sunday school, or
worship to affect their life-style. What is heard does not
translate into action, unless such action will be advantageous to
a personal concern or to manipulate others. It is distressing that
ethnic prejudice has been found to be more "common among
churchgoers than among nonchurchgoers. . . .The self is not
extended; there is no warm relating of self to others."[2]

It is a fact that for these veneered Christians, Scripture,
tradition, and teachings of the faith are held neatly in one hand,
while the reality of daily action is held in the other. The two
hands, at a distance from each other, do not touch! What an
immense frustration it is to hear them quote Scripture,
inevitably in righteous judgment of others, while disregarding
personal internalizing of the Word.

On Sunday, the message is "Thou shalt not steal." On
Monday, the expense account may be padded, a customer

shortchanged, or the employer's time wasted. Maybe these persons think that as long as they don't rob a bank, you can't be called thieves. If a faint voice does tell them that what they are doing is wrong, they easily justify what they do by saying, "Everyone else does it!" or "My boss doesn't appreciate me; I'm giving more than I should already." The speck in the eye of the world is clearly seen, despite blindness due to the log in the eye of the beholder (see Luke 6:41-42).

One manifestation of the hypocritical Christian is the successful-living mentality: "I wouldn't have the cars, the right friends, or productive business contacts if God didn't want me to have them." Whitewashing attempts to cover the iniquity, noisy songs, and rapacity. Faith is stunted because it is one of leftover childhood perceptions, when the ability to interpret the world is greatly limited. God is Santa Claus or an "overindulgent father" who "favors the immediate interests of the individual,"[3] or God is experienced as being highly erratic, requiring appeasement with good works, empty sacrifices.

I suspect that extrinsic religion can make one emotionally compulsive, trading a socially unacceptable compulsion for one that society condones. A friend described her "conversion" as one in which she used religion to quit drinking. "There was nothing indwelling," she could admit. "I was getting really obnoxious, trying to save people with whom I worked. Thanks be to God, I fell again and got normal." Oddly enough, starting to drink again helped sober her up to the recognition of the superficiality of her first commitment. Now she is well on her way to a life of abstinence.

People with an addiction can claim conversion before having any understanding of the compulsions in their lives. At first, my friend's uncontrolled devotion to drinking was changed to another uncontrolled devotion: religious fanaticism. This can happen to anyone, when living to drink or to work, to eat or to gamble is transferred into sanctimonious hypocrisy. You might say that is a decided improvement, and I am inclined to agree, until I think about people who beat others over the head with a Bible. It can be hellish in a household with a super Christian.

And much harm can be done to the person who is seeking a better way in seeing the extrinsic Christian try to serve two masters: God on Sunday, and the world on Monday through Saturday.

My experience as a prison chaplain has given me firsthand knowledge of "miracle" deliverance from addictive behavior to fireball evangelists. They can nearly drive you crazy with their newest obsession. Any life crisis has the potential for positive life reorientation. But if newly converted persons are not willing to be nurtured beyond the Santa Claus/Bogey Man immaturity, they are destined to spiritually dead pharisaism or becoming evangelical junkies. In a society that is increasingly escapist in a myriad of addictions, quick fixes, and "just pray about it" glibness, religion must not be marketed or accepted as a miracle cure-all.

There is a better way! Kierkegaard's term is the radical Christian. Such a faith requires that an individual interact and be changed by a community of believers who are grounded in the teachings of Jesus. Integration of beliefs and values with daily activity is sought.[3] That is clearly the opposite of donning a set of values, like a different dress or suit, according to the taste and goals of the day. Instead, intrinsic Christianity yearns for all aspects of life and learning to be in harmony. The result is holistic living.

When life is fully integrated, the two hands mentioned earlier, one holding the Word and the other holding attitude/action, open up and start informing each other. When your faith fashions your life, you don't wait for everyone else to shape up first. You get yourself in order. Then amazingly, others appear to be getting themselves together. It is never too late to start applying the Christian faith as we are seeking an authentic spirituality. One important way to do so is simple, and it works. Daily confession is the antidote for stockpiling sins. The admission should be specific and—when advisable, not incurring or compounding the hurt—should be admitted to the person or persons affected by our sinfulness.

I have been practicing the discipline of concrete and timely confession. At first, it seemed that I had to monitor every other thought and then make a confession. Arrogance, pride, the desire to be right, and perfectionism were at the top of my list. I have also had to guard against spiritual laziness in my confessions. It is easier and less traumatic if I say quickly, "I am sorry," but do not examine and own up to my specific guilt. It is humbling to say, "I admit that, in my wish to be right, I have totally discounted your feelings or perspective. I am sorry!" But the peace of mind from letting go of wounded pride makes it worthwhile. Acknowledgment of personal inadequacy and responsibility requires honesty, or guilt will be projected onto others. It has been spiritually invigorating for me to realize that as I have continued to monitor my thoughts and be unflinchingly honest, the occasions for confession have decreased, and I have reached a temporary plateau on the spiral of my faith journey.

Another practice that sorts out the infinite from the finite is developing and maintaining a sense of humor. When life is getting too somber or discouraging, I grab a laugh by seeking the humorous, from reading a comic strip to making a face at myself in the mirror.

The person of faith is in a wonderful position for having a "superior sense of humor" because that person has "settled once and for all what things are sacred and of ultimate value."[5] Then nothing else needs to be taken with utmost seriousness. What a freedom!

Being a lifelong learner is another hedge against religiosity. We will go to the grave, and then to our new life, with unanswered questions. In the meantime, we should be seekers, never afraid that new knowledge will upset outdated or immature thinking. Learning is not mental edema, but absorption of truths, leading to change in ourselves, great or small.

In varying ways, I have asserted that selfishness is a hallmark of the extrinsically religious, always expecting the payback.

The religion of the extrinsic Christian is a whitewash of works righteousness. There is, even in altruism, the risk of doing the right thing for the wrong reasons. Some people get an emotional high in the midst of their fine, benevolent work, saying, "It makes me feel good!" But the center of devotion must be God, not self. Feeling good is not the measure of servanthood.

Our movement toward integrity of life must ultimately involve working for the betterment of others, for bringing justice into the lives of hurting people. Micah, a prophet of the Southern Kingdom, tells us that "ten thousand rivers of oil" and the sacrifice of the firstborn are not pleasing to God. God pleads with and for the people for substance in fidelity, not cheap sacrifice. Micah says that God has plainly enunciated what is good: doing justice, lovingkindness, and walking humbly with God (see Mic. 6:8).

Finally, if we are to grow as committed Christians, we require guidance from God for all our efforts. Whether the inspiration, instruction, or advice comes directly from God through Scripture, other sacred writings, or from the person who appears to be the least in tune with God, an attitude of humility and vulnerability will enable us to perceive the will of God.

A simple, yet profound, prayer by thirteenth-century bishop Richard of Chichester reminds us of what Christ accomplished on our behalf and what we in gratitude should do day by day:

Thanks be to thee, Lord Jesus Christ,
for all the benefits which thou hast won for us,
for all the pains and insults which thou hast borne for us.
O most merciful Redeemer,
Friend and Brother,
may we know thee more clearly,
love thee more dearly,
and follow thee more nearly,
day by day.

NOTES

1. See Gordon W. Allport, *Pattern and Growth in Personality* (New York: Holt, Rinehart, and Winston, 1964), p. 300.

2. Ibid.

3. Ibid.

4. Ibid., p. 301. One is moving toward the end itself, not one's own ends.

5. Ibid.

Through prayer, study, and meditation, we strive in step 11 to improve conscious contact with God, as we pray for knowledge of God's will and the power to carry that out.

> *If you love him, why not serve him?*
> *If you love him, why not serve him?*
> *If you love him, why not serve him?*
> *Soldiers of the cross.*

TEN

OUR LIVES FRAMED BY PRAYER

In the musical *Fiddler on the Roof,* Tevye, the main character, speaks and sings of tradition in his native Russia. Traditions, he says, help us to "keep our balance." There are traditions regarding sleeping, eating, work and even the clothes we wear. Tevye explains that the Jewish people wear the prayer shawl because it shows their constant devotion to God.

In the song "If I Were a Rich Man," Tevye converses easily with God, even chiding God about not giving him worldly status. He has no problem requesting a modest fortune from God, after lamely acknowledging that poverty is not necessarily an embarrassing condition. Dreaming out loud of the wonderful life the wealth would bring, Tevye begins and ends his daydream by talking with God. Tevye's frustrations and hopes are framed by his relationship with God. At the end of the song, Tevye asks, "Would it spoil some vast, eternal plan, if I were a wealthy man?" No booming heavenly voice responds to Tevye's not-so-modest proposal. So, noting the setting sun, he goes into his home to begin the Sabbath with his family, reciting the traditional prayers he learned in childhood.

As engaging as Tevye's praying and talking to God are, we don't have to be creators of well-polished phrases to be able to talk with God. Opportunities to pray, from a breath prayer—a short prayer uttered as one inhales and exhales, such as "God, give me strength"—to one of greater length, can be anywhere, anytime, and under any circumstance. Jesus taught us how, when, and where to pray.

Early in Jesus' ministry, he had no trouble drawing a crowd. Persons sick in body and those possessed with demons or evil spirits clamored for his healing power. The curious and the doubtful eagerly sought him. In chapter 5 of Luke, the crowd was large and getting pushy. A nearby boat was used as a less pressing stage from which Jesus could teach. The demand for Jesus grew, and people came to him in increasing numbers: "But he withdrew to the wilderness and prayed" (Luke 5:16 RSV).

Jesus' statement can easily be upstaged by or appear to interrupt the moment of the marvelous teaching and healing and calling of disciples. It is not as spectacular as the two stories surrounding Jesus' retreat to pray: the cleansing of the leper or the healing of the paralyzed man. It is not clever or witty like Jesus' response to his critics, who loved to point out Jesus' sinful associates. But without the practice of prayer the resulting closeness with God, depth of commitment, and power to act would have been unattainable. In one short verse between exciting and miraculous acts, Luke tells us, "But [Jesus] would go away to lonely places, where he prayed" (Luke 5:16 GNB).

The sought-after, faith-nealing Rabbi goes from being a director who initiates action to being a star offstage, listening intently to the director in preparation for the critical role he was to fulfill. He was disposing himself to God's instruction for his life, deriving sustenance from being in the presence of God. This is not prayer as an afterthought, a reprieve or life insurance. It is, as Tevye reveals in his prayer, the frame around one's life.

It is no accident that we read of Jesus at prayer. He prayed with a purpose. Through prayer, he made decisions, was revitalized, and received God's power. The first of these, praying for preparation or decision making, is described in Luke 6 as Jesus prays before choosing the apostles: "In these days he went out to the mountain to pray; and all night he continued in prayer to God. And when it was day, he called his disciples, and chose from them twelve, whom he named apostles" (Luke 6:12-13 RSV). After Jesus prayed, there was almost always a change. It may have been a change in locale, or it may have been an important action taken by him. Through prayer, he was able to perceive God's will and then to act on it. Jesus, God's Son, needed to pray!

Ernest Gordon's book *Through the Valley of the Kwai* tells of the power that comes through prayer. The book reveals the story of 76,000 English and American POWs and Southeast Asians who died in Thailand as they struggled against unrelenting obstacles of starvation, heat, and brutality to build a railroad. Those obstacles brought out the most depraved actions of the POWs. When they could sink no lower, the example and courage of Christians in the camp gradually became the leaven for repentance, conversion, and recommitment. They began to seek to emulate Jesus Christ's life and sacrificial death. As they studied and worshiped together, the captives "stumbled over the phrase" in the Lord's Prayer: "And forgive us our debts as we also have forgiven our debtors." They stumbled because to live that prayer meant forgiving their captors.[3] That prayer began to sustain them as well as direct their thinking. They prayed in all circumstances, regardless of the situation, even as they were beaten. Those who had become the church were praying! The realization came that "God makes neighbors; we make enemies."[4]

The men found that when the easy route is not possible, or that evil is for the moment in control, if we go through the ordeal relying on God's Spirit and power, we can be victorious. Jesus' growing popularity tested his mission. To maintain his direction, he had to move away from the acclamation of the crowds for communion with God. That was a time of contemplation and resting in God, which prepared Jesus to be God's instrument of healing.

Many of us are in environments that are polluted by noise. We must find a quiet space and allow ourselves to be restored through resting in God. It may be only a moment or two, and we may have to find that calm within ourselves when the situation does not allow our physically leaving an area, but if we turn ourselves toward God, the result can be a renewing of body and spirit.

Nicholas Herman was known as Brother Lawrence after he became a lay brother in the Carmelite order in the seventeenth century. He learned to practice God's presence by impressing on his heart and convincing his mind of God's divine existence. He stated that by a continual practice, "I am come to a state wherein it would be as difficult for me not to think of God as it was at first to accustom myself to it." You might guess that Brother Lawrence had great amounts of time in which to accomplish his goal. Actually, he was assigned to the kitchen of the monastery to cook for the community. Amid pots, pans, potatoes, bread, and other distractions, he kept two levels of consciousness: one was to his duties and the other was to his God-awareness. At the end of each day, he took an inventory of himself. If he had been successful, he thanked God. If Brother Lawrence had failed to any degree of his God-awareness, he made amends with God and picked up the discipline again, "as if he had never deviated from it." How much more productive that is than self-pity or endless mental haranguing.[1]

A third purpose for Jesus to pray was to receive God's power. There is no more poignant, heartbreaking scene than his praying alone the night of his betrayal. Jesus prayed for the cup to be taken away from him, but only if it were the will of his Father (see Matt. 26:36-46; Mark 14:32-42; Luke 22:40-46). Jesus returned to the disciples a strong, committed Son, ready to do the bidding of his heavenly parent. Instead of being saved from the brutalities and torture facing him, he was given power to endure and thereby overcome them.

Some people appear to be confident in knowing God's will for their lives. I have not found it so easy. I can see how I have grown in my desire to *do* the will of God. At times in the past, I feared that my will and God's will would not mesh, so to seek to know God's plan was a risky enterprise. My usual experience now is to pray and pray, and not to lose heart in continued praying. That is decidedly more for my benefit than for God. My awarenes of that particular prayer and desire for direction help me to identify God's answer when it comes, especially if it is not in the form I had anticipated or desired. If we have not spent time in getting to know God, it is possible that we will not recognize God's answer to that prayer.

At times only in retrospect can I recognize God's answer. On other occasions, I have recognized God's response to my prayers immediately, even when the answer was other than my exact specification. There have been times when, quite unexpectedly, an idea came to mind in a fully articulated sentence, which I was sure was from God.

In October of 1972, my husband and I, with our seventeen-month-old son, moved to Texas after we had spent three years in Germany. It was a difficult winter, adjusting to everything from new jobs to new germs; our resistance was low. One winter morning, we all awoke feeling nauseated. My husband managed to get up, shave unsteadily, and go to the church where he was an associate pastor. After a while, he called to see how we were doing and to report that he was feeling better. I asked him whether something might be wrong with our heating system. He didn't think there was a problem, but he suggested I crack a window for ventilation. I lay back down, our son sound asleep beside me.

I was in that time between waking and sleeping, and I suddenly knew, without question, that we must get out of the house. Shakily, but with as much speed as possible, I dressed myself and grabbed our little boy. I ran to the neighbors' house, collapsing on their front porch. I cannot explain the strong, impelling directive to leave the house, except to say that God spoke to me. I do not mean that I heard a voice, but I knew what I had to do to save myself and our son. That afternoon, we learned that, indeed, there was a malfunction of the heating system and that our bodies had been filling with deadly carbon monoxide. That knowledge did not come from me. In my dreamlike state, God got through to me!

Jesus demonstrated his need for direction, rest, and power.

The models are not descriptions of, or occasions for, public prayer. They are examples for us of intimate times with God, not to impress another, but to commune with our creator.

Jesus' teaching on prayer strictly warns against hypocrisy: "And when you pray, you must not be like the hypocrites; for they love to stand and pray in the synagogues and at the street corners, that they may be seen by men" (Matt. 6:5 RSV). A Hasidic saying confirms the private observance of prayer: One kind of love of God is the "love spent in learning and praying and fulfilling the commandments, which should be shown in silence and not in the presence of others, lest it tempt to glory and pride."[2]

Jesus did not seek the cross, but he sought God's will and received the power to endure the cross. Jesus demonstrated a life rich in its intimate relationship with God. Brother Lawrence described how one can practice being in God's presence. The prisoners of war began to live a life of prayer through Bible study.

Communing with God in order to have our lives delineated by God takes effort, time, and discipline. As we practice it, we will find that our decisions are no longer completely ours, but are directed by God. We will be able to be renewed by God's presence. We will receive the strength to carry us beyond our human limitations. A life that is framed by a practice of prayer is also a life that spirals around a consciousness of God, giving us the essence as well as the boundary for our whole being.

NOTES

1. Herman Nicholas, *The Practice of the Presence of God* (New York: Fleming H. Revell, 1895), pp. 28-30.

2. Martin Buber, *Ten Rungs: Hasidic Sayings* (New York: Schocken Books, 1947), p. 21.

3. Ernest Gordon, *Through the Valley of the Kwai* (New York: Harper, 1962), p. 213.

4. Ibid., p. 222.

How happy is one who reaches step 12, for it describes a spiritual awakening. As the result of these steps, we carry the message of God's love, grace, and forgiveness to other sinners like ourselves and endeavor to practice these principles in our life.

> *We are climbing higher, higher;*
> *We are climbing higher, higher,*
> *We are climbing higher, higher;*
> *Soldiers of the cross.*

ELEVEN

TOP OF THE GUEST LIST

A city in the United States faced a problem that was plaguing many metropolitan areas: the growing number of street people—children and their mothers, men and women. Citizen complaints ranged from fear of the safety of the streets to an outcry from those who were shocked that society had failed to provide at least a minimal standard of living and sanitation to all. A study was ordered, and to no one's surprise the conclusion was that new programs needed to be implemented and temporary shelter provided. Fortunately, funding for shelters was available because Mrs. Albritton—a woman of considerable means, who was known for her philanthropy—generously promised to be the chief grantor of money.

A knowledgeable and experienced staff from among social service agencies and representative homeless persons was assembled. Early on, Judy—who had been evicted from her home and lived on the streets with her two children—was identified as one who could speak to persons in positions of authority and to those whose lives appeared to be beyond their control. The newly created agency became a team of persons dedicated to eradicating both the causes and the occasions for homelessness. Immediate and total elimination of the roots was impossible, but persons who followed the program, doubters and believers, all said the Commission to Abrogate Street People (CASP) was well on its way to providing a national prototype. That did not escape the attention of the nation's President. He was so delighted that he decided to visit the city to learn more about the program and to host a dinner honoring all who had been involved in it. A part of the evening would be to choose and recognize the person who most epitomized the achievement of CASP. Mrs. Albritton, philanthropist extraordinaire, was thrilled beyond words.

The guest list was compiled, and invitations were sent. At the head table sat the director, Mrs. Albritton, and city dignitaries. Scattered throughout the convention hall were members of the staff, media, concerned citizens, and many street people. Judy was at a table far removed from the head table, sitting with friends from her days on the streets and with her colleagues from work.

Mrs. Albritton did not pass up the opportunity for a new gown, and she felt fine indeed on the night of the banquet. She commented to persons around her that it was an honor merely to shake the President's hand. Fully anticipating being recipient of the recognition plaque, she had written a brief speech and memorized it so that note cards were unnecessary.

The President was introduced, and the crowd broke into enthusiastic applause. His speech revealed that a script writer had facts and the spirit of CASP, and the President's extemporaneous remarks proved him well-informed also. His praise was extensive and heady. "But there is one," he said, "who stands out, whose compassion, generosity, and vision have been a model for all and who epitomizes the transformation in this city's homeless."

Mrs. Albritton placed her napkin on the table and positioned her feet, inwardly rehearsing surprise.

The President continued, "So I ask Judith Maxine Jackson to come to the podium to receive a plaque to express the gratitude of this city and our nation."

Perfunctory applause was immediate, but raucous applause broke out at Judy's table. The honoree did not move.

A co-worker looked at her in astonishment, "Judy, the President called out your name. Go to the podium to receive your award!"

"Me?" Judy questioned.

Everyone at the table was saying, "Yes, yes, you!"

As Judy made her way through tables and chairs to the front of the banquet hall, Mrs. Albritton looked ashen and shaken. Suddenly, she realized that everyone was standing, and she clumsily rose to her feet, the fluid, graceful movements of rising and approaching the President completely forgotten.

Shaking the President's hand, Judy accepted the plaque. Then she spoke to the group: "I can receive this award only as I accept it on behalf of many, many people: my supervisor, people who became family while we lived on the streets, my co-workers." Turning to Mrs. Albritton, Judy said, "We all owe a debt of gratitude to our benefactor, whose unselfish generosity has meant the freedom to implement a reformation in our city. It is good to pause here and celebrate how far we have come, but our present triumph should not dull our awareness that the job is not yet complete. Tonight there are people with no beds, suffering physically and mentally, whose lives are at risk. Tomorrow we continue what has been well begun." She raised the plaque over her head, and only the sound of cameras catching the moment could be heard. Tears were highlighted on Judy's cheeks. "I salute you all!" she said.

A newspaper headline the next day read, "Humility Marks Recipient of President's Award." Unfortunately for Mrs. Albritton, one reporter had her camera trained on the benefactor, snapping a telling shot as the President called out the name of Judith Maxine Jackson. The photo was not flattering.

One sabbath when Jesus went to dine at the house of a ruler who belonged to the Pharisees, they were watching him.

Noticing how they chose the places of honor, Jesus told a parable to those who were invited, saying to them. "When you are invited by any one to a marriage feast, do not sit down in a place of honor, lest a more eminent person than you be invited; and the one who invited you both will come and say to you, 'Give place to this person,' and then you will begin with shame to take the lowest place. But when you are invited, go and sit in the lowest place, so that your host, having come, may say to you, 'Friend, go up higher'; then you will be honored in the presence of all who sit at table with you. For all who exalt themselves will be humbled, and all who humble themselves will be exalted."

Jesus said also to the person who had invited him, "When you give a dinner or a banquet, do not invite your friends or your brothers and sisters or your relatives or rich neighbors, lest they also invite you in return, and you be repaid. But when you give a feast, invite those who are poor and maimed and lame and blind, and you will be blessed, because they cannot repay you. You will be repaid at the resurrection of the just." (Luke 14:1, 7-14 ILL)

In a seminary course I took, the final exam was a project, the synopsis of which was to be presented after the class had dinner at the professor's home. Whether it was meanness or a stroke of genius on my part, you may decide. I asked the professor if a simulation could be part of my project. After I described it, she graciously agreed.

This was the plan: I convinced the pastor of the church where I was working not to shave for a day or two. He was then to come to the professor's house while we were preparing the meal and ask for food. We would be treated to a hard-luck story in the bargain. (What a supervising pastor! His transformation from Sunday vestments to pauper attire was remarkable.) It worked like a charm. I am still amazed that no one suspected a setup. Right on schedule, he appeared. I played my part, asking the professor whether the vagrant might be given something to eat. I suggested that we exhibit Christian charity and invite him to eat with us. Since I had answered the door and appealed his case, I should sit near him. Our table was rather quiet, so I began talking with our guest street person. Later, others described my conversation as being more like an interrogation than a dinner chat.

Soon after the meal he disappeared into the night, and we got down to the business of reports. There was nearly a riot when I revealed my "paper." One student was particularly incensed. "I worried the whole time he was here that he was casing our professor's house and would be back later to rob her. I had already planned to offer to stay over the night." Then he turned and looked me in the eye, "That was a pretty dirty trick you played on us!"

My expectation had been that the whole role-play would be quickly discovered and we would have a good laugh. Then a deep and soul-baring discussion would ensue about our tendency—the more the shame because we called ourselves Christians—to judge by outward appearances. Never did I dream that a reaction of anger would predominate. I believe the student's pride was injured because he had been "tricked" and in his own mind made to look foolish. Rather than using the incident to reflect on his own reaction, he lashed out at me. I cannot know definitely, but I would hope that if the tables had been turned I would have acknowledged any arrogance and been chagrined at my judgment of someone on the basis of economics. Any anger should have been at myself, not at the one who held the mirror up to my face.

Christians are not immune to and experience susceptibility to conceit, vanity, and pride. Recognizing and admitting sinfulness is a humbling awakening, but as we get more biblical knowledge, attend church more faithfully, give more generously, evangelize more ardently, and pray more eloquently, the chasm between the saint and the sinner widens to a chasm, and pride starts rearing its seductive head. Anyone who says that pride has never been a problem for him or her is too prideful to admit it has.

There is a delightful turnabout in the story from Luke. The guests were watching Jesus at dinner. But it was Jesus who accurately saw them. The simple choice of a place to sit gave him the occasion to point out how they revealed their perceived self-importance by assuming the seats of honor. You would think they would have known better. The problem with pride is that it usually knows the least because it is deaf to criticism.

The little book of Obadiah is the shortest in the Old Testament. The writing is a strong indictment of the Edomites and tells of their destruction. Their wisdom (v. 8) and might (v. 9) will not protect them, for the pride in their hearts has duped them. In this book, which cautions against the downfall of the haughty, humility is personified in the writer's anonymity. Whether through intention or an accident of history, the prophet's low profile makes a good case for his humility.

> Behold, I will make you small
>> among the nations,
>> you shall be utterly despised.
> *The pride of your heart has*
>> *deceived you,*
>> you who live in the clefts of the
>> rock,
>> whose dwelling is high,
> who say in your heart,
>> "Who will bring me down to the
>> ground?"
> Though you soar aloft like the eagle,
>> though your nest is set among the
>> stars,
>> thence I will bring you down,
>>> says the Lord.
> (Obad. 1:2-4 RSV; italics added)

Beautiful, soaring eagles with nests in the stars will be brought low by that which is higher: God! Pride is the prelude of destruction (see Prov. 16:18-19).

Being around small children can give one lessons in humility. Out of the innocence of their young years, thoughts and speech are uncensored, from "That's not a pretty dress" to "You need to do something with your hair; it looks awful!" Maybe it's the voice of God—not about our clothing or hair—but about us, telling us not to treat ourselves with utmost seriousness. It has been said that angels can fly because they take themselves lightly.

Persons who have high visibility in our culture are susceptible to an inflated sense of self. They maintain that conceit by surrounding themselves with flatterers and yes-people. But

Jesus kindly gives us the advice that if we place ourselves first, embarrassment will be waiting around the corner.

Whatever noble attributes we have, talents we are endowed with, or accomplishments we have attained, it is our place to exalt God, and it is God's place to exalt those who are humble.

Dear Mrs. Albritton, she soared for a time among the stars, but she was brought down to the ground. Judy's rise was gracious. Both had worked diligently, and thanks were in order. Judy was in the service of others. Mrs. Albritton served primarily herself; she had her reward in earthly praise.

Here's my suggestion for Mrs. Albritton's memorized speech: "I want to thank God for allowing me the privilege of being a servant." That is the message to carry to others by how we live: Christians serve.

TWELVE

THE SONG OF THE GOOD

Tryouts were held for a melodrama with its stereotypical good and evil characters. I wanted the part of the shady lady, Ritzie. I wanted to sink my teeth into a part that would epitomize the dark side and reveal my ability to capture it. The shady lady was more interesting than the heroine! An acquaintance of mine wanted the role of the flawless heroine, Miss Ivory. We confided in each other about the roles we would "die" for, and I secretly breathed a sigh of relief that we were not competing for the same part. True to melodramatic style, the heroine's character was flat and non-engaging. Ritzie had all the good lines! My heart and soul yearned for Ritzie, but the director judged otherwise. I won the non-coveted role of Miss Ivory, and, of course, my acquaintance received the prized role of Ritzie!

Have you ever seen a movie or play or read an absorbing novel and been jubilant when the worst wins out? You may pause a moment, chagrined at your feelings. But the evil forces, with their depth of character development and dramatic lines, placed alongside the banality of the good, contribute to a fascinating figure. It has been said that no great scoundrel is ever uninteresting. Isn't the good, the beautiful, the pure, the enticing more alluring than evil?

The mythical Isle of Sirens is one of those places you wouldn't want to go on vacation. It was inhabited by

103

creatures—part female, part bird—whose beguiling singing was an enticement to sailors. Absolutely mesmerized by the sound, they would leap from their ships and swim to shore, only to be devoured by the Sirens.

Two Greek heroes, Odysseus, King of Ithaca—whom the Romans called Ulysses—and Orpheus, poet and musician, each by necessity sailed past the Isle of Sirens.

As Odysseus approached the Isle, he instructed his sailors to put wax in their ears, and he ordered them to tie him to the mast. During the harrowing stretch past the song of the Sirens, Odysseus had to be bound even tighter with stronger ropes to prevent his bursting loose, for his soul craved the song.

An entirely different tactic saved Orpheus and his crew. He used his gifts of poetry and song to pay homage to gods and goddesses. On the voyage with his fellow Argonauts, Orpheus sat calmly, playing his lyre and singing as they passed the Isle. His music was so splendid that the Argonauts paid no attention to the Sirens. The ship passed on without losing a man, and without the trauma of a contest of wills. The appearance of loveliness in the Sirens' melodies was overcome by the reality of beauty in Orpheus' music.

Now that's how I think it should be: the superficial appeal of evil, the transitory desire for that which is eventually destructive is overcome by the purity of the good and authentically beautiful. Sailors fell unwittingly into the snare of the Sirens. Odysseus and Orpheus both knew this, but their defenses were strikingly different. The crew and Odysseus escaped, but it was torture for them. Orpheus' music could charm lions and tigers, draw out shy animals of the forest, and animate trees and rocks. Even the water flowed with a hush. Orpheus was more at home offering his song to bring harmony to the wilderness than in public entertainment, but it is because he gave his music to others that his song was efficacious. In order to overcome the song of the Sirens in your life, you must listen to the song of the good.

When Bible stories are retold, often the absorbing portrayals are the Jezebels and the Judases. With grand gestures and raw emotions, they are etched in our minds. Exploring their actions can help us to perceive better our own capacity for evil.

But how long has it been since you read or saw a portrayal of Christ that captivated you? Unfortunately, writers have been capitalizing on a genuine interest and faith in Jesus and the events of his life by concocting bizarre stories, questioning Jesus' conduct, motives, or sanity. Maybe we believe the expression, "It's too good to be true." Maybe Jesus couldn't have been all that holy! A docetist would disclaim any expression of emotions by Jesus. That is not my belief. I believe that Jesus was tempted and experienced intense feelings.

Imaginative depictions of the lives of Jesus and his contemporaries help us to connect and converse with them over the centuries. Many have noted, and rightly so, that the movie *The Last Temptation of Christ*—which is based on the book of the same title by Nikos Kazantzakis—is a mirror for ourselves. But Jesus' nature is more exploited than explored, so that Jesus becomes the antithesis of himself. In the movie, Jesus observes of Judas, "Of all my friends you are the strongest." Judas, the hero, directs the life of a weakling Jesus.

What is Judas about in *The Last Temptation of Christ*? He is taken off the hook as the betrayer. Judas' lack of understanding of or belief in Jesus is explained by Jesus' pleading with Judas to betray him. Judas had earlier warned Jesus that if he strayed the least little bit from the vaguely defined mission, Judas would kill Jesus. Finally, Jesus confesses to Judas that he has strayed—presumably from not overthrowing the Romans—and that Judas has no choice but to turn him in. For those who have yet to comprehend a "Judas," Jesus' collusion with Judas is a tempting solution. But a fictionalized, unstable Jesus, who waffles between love and the sword, and a Judas who often yells reduce Jesus' life and sacrifice to a pathetic attempt at profundity.

The depiction in the movie of corruption as appealing in its disguises is on target. The satanic being in the dancing fire, who tempts Jesus, and the child-guardian angel—later revealed to be the satan—who drew Jesus from the cross are visually appealing—and therein lies the danger. There are two distinct problems in identifying and confronting evil. The first is that it often comes elegantly wrapped in the exact size of our most craved wish. Who wouldn't make a 180 degree turn if suddenly a flaming red, long-tailed figure with a pitchfork poised for tossing materialized in front of him or her? Things and people are seldom what they initially appear to be! The second problem is that decency and honesty are commonly perceived as being sickly and pale in comparison to the vibrancy and excitement of the profane.

Evil is as real as roses and gardens. It is a peddler of hate and pain, and we should never underestimate that it is an expert in disguises. To ignore evil mindlessly is to let it run unchecked in the world or to give it power over our lives—even though its power is minuscule compared to God's strength. We construct a back door to avoid facing the truth at the front door. Saying "the devil made me do it" is a temporary anesthesia. Sirach declares wisely:

> When an ungodly man curses his
>   adversary,
>   he curses his own soul.
> (Sir. 21:27 RSV)

I could go on endlessly about evil, horror movies, and Sirens. Should I continue in that vein, I would do precisely what I wish to argue against: immersing the reader in the malevolence that automatically blocks the cultivation of the holy.

Instead, I want us to grasp the radical nature of the goodness of Christ and to seek that goodness in life. We know of the temptations Jesus faced, and we know that he did not sin. Harry Emerson Fosdick tells us that evil passions are overcome by stronger passions and that the "soul unoccupied by a positive devotion is sure to be occupied by spiritual demons." He continues: "The safety of the Master in the presence of temptation lay in his complete and positive devotion to his mission; there was no unoccupied room in his soul where evil could find a home; he knew . . . 'The expulsive power of a new affection.' "[1]

The Siren song, judged by most to be lyrically beautiful, was actually discordant when Orpheus' music was on the wind. Jesus' life "of positive goodness, so full, so glad, so triumphant . . . conquered sin by surpassing it."[2]

What do we learn when we look at Jesus? Jesus' sacrificial death is the crowning act of his earthly life. It is believable to us because we have a record of how he lived. Jesus demonstrated compassion and love for all people, not limiting himself to one blood line or being inattentive to particular concerns for children and women. He worked with great dedication, but he recognized that time was needed apart from others, especially time spent with his heavenly parent. Jesus saw potential in unlikely people and spoke directly when the occasion was appropriate, calling all to the highest spiritual commitment. But he allowed people to say no. He enjoyed being in community with his disciples (who numbered far more than twelve) and with other saints and sinners. His many healings and feeding of the crowd showed his awareness and concern for the physical needs of others. He had stamina and strength, and he faced his adversaries squarely without belittling them or giving ground—all without violence and show of force. He shared his power and authority unselfishly. Jesus was strong and gentle, a servant and a savior. He loved without regard for reward. He forgave to heal the world. His goodness defined the meaning of good.

As goodness becomes more and more both our goal and our daily expression, we are being prepared to share our knowledge, conviction, and commitment to others. It is expected of us. One of the last words spoken by Jesus to the disciples was that through the Holy Spirit they would be empowered to be witnesses to the world.

How do we tell others of our good news? To follow in the example of Christ, Christians ought to have charisma. We should be appealing to others as they study us and remark: "There is strength in that person which I do not know; there is courage which I have never exhibited; there is dynamic love which I have never expressed." Those who study us to see whether we are real should discover that the more they study the more they learn of God. We should be sought for our wisdom. We should set the moral tone of home, work, and school. Whether standing or bending over to meet the need of another, we can happily give of ourselves. Our light can shine for those who have become accustomed to the dark.

We must articulate the faith as well. Although persuasive and ardent, our speech should also be gentle and winsome. The evangelist who condemns others, listing sins and sinners, is not telling the good news, but is driving away the seeker. We should persevere as much in our praying that God will prepare the way as in praying that God will lead us to be useful servants. Finally, we must guard against arrogance. If we are humbly aware of our own shortcomings and sinfulness, we don't have so far to fall, and fall we will from time to time. If we understand relapses as part of recovery or sinning as part of growing in strength to overcome what separates us from God, we can truthfully speak of opportunities for growth, not of failure.

Should we despair that wrongdoers appear to have nine lives, always landing on their feet? Not if we believe that wrongdoing is abhorrent to the quintessence of right doing:

> Fret not yourself because of the wicked,
> be not envious of wrongdoers!
> For they will soon fade like the grass,
> and wither like the green herb.
> Trust in God . . . and *do good*;
> so you will dwell in the land, and enjoy security.
> Take delight in God . . .
> who will give you the desires of your heart.
> Commit your way to God . . .
> trust in God, and God will act.
> (Ps. 37:1-5 ILL; italics added)

As loved, forgiven, and reborn people, we should love and exemplify forgiveness. Melodies more exquisite than those of the Sirens should pour from our mouths in praise of God and in building bridges of relationships, drawing those who hear closer and closer to God's beauty and goodness, until they behold the wonders of God's love.

It is easy enough to see the dark, the corrupt. But the song of the good abounds in this world:

—a sunrise reflected in the eyes of the church gathered for an Easter service;
the baptism of an infant, an adult, a child;
the ethereal music of a chanting congregation;
a father holding and comforting a crying child;
a female pastor celebrating the Eucharist;
a worshiper sensing God's transcendence and majesty in the hallowed space of a Gothic cathedral;
two hands held, petitioning God for strength;
liturgical dancers, stretching sinews and muscles in praise of God;
handbells rung by inmates who are free in Christ;
a sunset firing sand and sea;
a starry night.

God's goodness extends into the creation of galaxies and into the creation of the minute. For all time, it can be said: "Behold, it [is] very good" (Gen. 1:31 RSV)!

I have changed. Ritzie, the role I so wanted to play, was indeed interesting—then. But now I am intrigued by the good. I rejoice when I see good overcoming evil—as the only possible victor. I am fascinated by characters in novels and plays, and by everyday people who defeat the evil that is within and without. The good and the beautiful draw us to it. Godliness is believable, engaging, and exciting.

An image that has been woven into these chapters is the spiral. The process of deepening spirituality has its forward movement and its regressions. But a spiral continues to cut through new planes. It is not a matter of who's above or who's below. There is no need for competition, which is the antithesis of spirituality. We need never feel that we have completely regressed to the beginnings of our journey. Once we have gained wisdom, practiced our faith, experienced faith, and lived repentance and reconciliation, we are not the same.

Tell someone who needs to hear the good news that God reigns with power and loving authority. Therefore, as children of the kingdom, although we falter, the God who is within us enlightens us; the God who is beside us comforts and accompanies us; the God who is beyond us beckons and encourages us on our spiraling journey.

All praise and thanks be to God.

NOTES

1. Harry Emerson Fosdick, *The Manhood of the Master* (New York: Association Press, 1920), p. 91.
2. Ibid.